FROM HELL TO THE PROMISED LAND

SAM SILBERBERG

ISBN-10: 1466218320
ISBN-13: 978-1466218321

ACKNOWLEDGEMENT

I want to thank John Miller of Portland, Oregon, for his support and encouragement in creating this testimony. He was there for me in the summer of 2000 when I relived my past experiences on our trip to Poland for the writing of this memoir. I must thank my daughter Ilana for her persistent urging that I get on with the job.

I thank Anne Clark, tutor and instructor of the Laguna Woods Village Macintosh Club, for the professional services she rendered. Anne has done a great job of formatting, editing and picture placement of this book. She is responsible for creating the PDF file of this book for submission to the publisher.

DEDICATION

This memoir is in honor of my wife Anita, our children David and Ilana, our grandchildren Jeremy and Jahnna whose lives have been affected by the shadow of the Holocaust. It is a tribute to our entire family and the six million Jews who were exterminated by the Nazis in the Holocaust during the Second World War of 1939 - 1945.

CONTENTS

PROLOGUE

I was born on August 25, 1929, in Jaworzno, Poland. My father and mother were orthodox Jews observing all religious traditions of Chasidic Judaism. (A Chasid is an orthodox Jew who follows the teachings of a particular rabbi). I was one of four children – three boys and one girl.

Our extended family in Jaworzno and the surrounding towns consisted of approximately 108 persons. Our family had roots in this area for many generations. The Silberberg clan was very hard working in various fields of endeavor. My grandfather owned a print shop and a stationery store, and he was a majority stockholder in a bus corporation servicing the line between Katowice in the west and Krakow in the east. My father had nine siblings, five brothers and four sisters. All of them were actively involved in the family's businesses.

My father and mother owned a men's clothing store, yet my father was working nights in the print shop his family owned. Jaworzno was a coal-mining town with a total population of 25,000 prior to WWII. There were 1,600 Jews living in Jaworzno, belonging to five different temples officiated by five different rabbis. In the Chasidic tradition, the rabbi is the final arbitrator in all disputes, business and family. The rabbi is also the sole interpreter of Jewish law. That gives him a revered status in the community of his followers.

My mother was busy helping my father in the business. I was nursed and raised by Julka, our Christian nanny, until I reached 3 years of age. In the fall of 1932, I attended cheder, an orthodox religious Hebrew school, from 9 a.m. to 4 p.m., with a break for lunch. The subjects taught at the cheder were how to read Hebrew prayer books and how to read the Torah (the five books of Moses). Only after we grasped the technique of reading the Hebrew words did we get a translation of their meaning. The language of instruction was Yiddish, an old Germanic language utilizing the Hebrew alphabet. Orthodox

Jews deemed Hebrew to be a Holy language, only to be used for prayer and liturgical purposes, not to be desecrated by daily usage.

Having been raised by a Christian nanny, I was at a total disadvantage. I did not know nor understand Yiddish or Hebrew. It was difficult for me to comprehend everything that the rabbi was saying. Gradually, I learned to speak Yiddish. My parents could no longer keep secrets from me by speaking Yiddish among themselves.

This routine continued until I was six years of age in the fall of 1935. It was also the time when my younger brother Ben-Zion (the Son of Zion) was born. In the fall of 1935, I started to attend public school from 8:30 a.m. to 12:30. I went home for lunch, and from 1:30 to 4:30 p.m., I attended cheder (Hebrew school). That pretty much rounded out my day at the age of 6. Between public school and cheder, I was kept pretty busy all week.

The Hebrew Sabbath is celebrated from sundown on Friday until after sundown on Saturday. It is totally devoted to family. On Friday afternoon, we would go with my father to take a Turkish bath and get dressed in our holiday outfits to go with my father for prayer services in the synagogue. After the prayer services we went to pay homage to our great-grandmother. She was seated at the head of a long table that was covered with white tablecloth, and was surrounded by the entire Silberberg clan all the way down to her great-grandchildren. Her oldest son would make the Kiddush, a prayer sanctifying the Sabbath over a glass of wine. She would then distribute candies to all her great-grandchildren, and we would all leave to our respective homes for the Sabbath meal. It is a memory I cherish to this day.

On the Sabbath, after the morning prayers and lunch it was time to take a nap. It was a tradition in our house that after the nap, one of my father's friends would come to our house and examine our knowledge of the week's Torah lessons. We made sure that we passed the test, otherwise, whatever little free time we had would be curtailed.

In public school, the majority of pupils were Catholics, which was the predominant religion of Poland. The Jewish children, who were a small minority, were constantly harassed and bullied by the Catholic children. We were called names such as Jew bastard, Christ killer, Jew Leper, etc. When I told my father about this bullying, he explained to me the history of the crucifixion of Jesus, which happened 2000 years ago, and told me that the Jews were not to blame for it. I resented being hassled over something that happened 2000 years ago that I had nothing to do with.

When I inquired into this problem in greater depth, I realized that the animosity of these kids stemmed from anti-Semitism instituted by their parents and the Catholic Church.

As long as it was limited to verbal abuse, I didn't mind. When they started to beat up Jewish children, I decided to stand up to them. I asked some Jewish children to gather in my house, which was near the school. We walked to school together, and when we were bullied by one of these kids I would not be afraid to fight him. They nicknamed me "grozny zydek" (the fearless Jew), which I didn't mind at all. I accepted it as a normal routine of life even though I did not like it.

The summer vacations we spent with my mother and Julka in the mountains. During the winter months, I loved sledding.

1   FALL OF 1937

It was the last week in August of 1937. My mother, two of my brothers, my sister and our nanny, were returning from summer vacation in the mountains. We would start another year of school and cheder (Hebrew school). For my sister Ruzia (Rachel), this was going to be her first year of school, while my older brother Moses David (Moniek) would start his first year of high school. Ben-Zion (the Son of Zion, nicknamed Benek), my youngest brother, was 5 years old and attended cheder school from 9 a.m. until 4:30 p.m. with an hour for lunch.

We had to cut our vacation short, because mother had to prepare the children for school. She also had to help my father in our clothing store, which was very busy selling new outfits for children for the new school year. In addition to all of this, she had to prepare everything for the celebration of the Rosh-Hashanah (the Jewish New-Year) and the high holidays, which start by mid September. This gave me the opportunity to hook up with my friends from school and cheder and find out how they spent their summer vacation and get updated on the latest events in town.

I heard that during the second week of September the Polish army would have maneuvers in town with all sorts of military equipment and artillery. I was excited about the upcoming maneuvers and was looking forward to watching them. In the days before the maneuvers began, we played various war games in the yards of our families and friends. Two days before Rosh-Hashanah, the maneuvers started. I was very excited to follow the tanks and armored vehicles into the fields and watch them conduct different war games with each other.

On the day before the holiday, as I was eagerly following the maneuvers, I felt a severe pain in my belly, but I was so involved in watching the maneuvers that I ignored my pain, hoping it would disappear. As time passed, the pain intensified, and I had to go home and go to bed. When my mother saw me lying in bed while the army was conducting maneuvers, she knew I must really be in pain. I could not join my father and my brothers to go to the synagogue for Rosh-Hashanah services. I was in so much pain that I could not join the family at the dinner table that evening. I had a sleepless night, and the following morning my mother went to the garden to bring some large green leaves to use as a compress on my belly with ice. My father went with my brothers to the synagogue. I kept moaning and groaning in excruciating pain. My mother went to fetch the doctor to check up on me. The doctor told my mother that I had a ruptured appendix and that this was an emergency and that I must be taken to a hospital in Krakow, which was about 50 kilometers from our town, Jaworzno.

My mother sent our nanny to the synagogue to fetch my father and inform him of the emergency, telling him that we must leave by bus to Krakow, which would leave the station within the next hour. My father, who was performing the mid-day prayer service, had to excuse himself from the worshipers and left to rush us to the bus terminal. The surgeon, who was also Jewish, had to be summoned on an emergency call to the hospital to perform the operation. Because the ruptured appendix was in a bad state, my parents were told that the success of the operation could not be guaranteed. I remember being hospitalized for a very long time with wads of cotton soaked with puss being pulled out of a large incision in my belly. I remember my grandfather at my bedside praying and reciting the Psalms of David for my successful recovery.

I guess his intervention worked and I recovered from my ordeal. Later that year, my grandmother Malka (my grandfather's wife) died. This was the first time I observed the entire Silberberg clan, consisting of 108 members, plus relatives from neighboring towns gather to pay homage to the matriarch of the family. It was the first time I was aware of death and did not quite know what to make of it. I saw the casket being lowered into the ground and people taking turns to shovel dirt onto it. I was told that I would never see grandma again because she had taken a journey to heaven.

In the spring of 1938, there was a huge wedding in my grandfather's house when my father's sister Sarah got married. This was a joyous occasion when the entire Silberberg clan and friends gathered to cheer the bride and groom and join in their celebration.

Aunt Sarah at her wedding in January 1939.

This was also when I got to know and play with my out-of-town cousins.

Shlomek, Benek, Janek, Shmilek, Shulek, Rose, Salushia.
Shulek in the back.

This picture of four generations of the Silberberg family
was taken at Aunt Sarah's wedding.

2 THE CLOUDS OF PERSECUTION

In the fall of 1938, a large bon-voyage party was given for my grandfather who was leaving Poland for Palestine to live in Jerusalem. It was a large gathering of family members and members of the congregation. There were many invited guests gathered to celebrate my grandfather's voyage to the "Promised Land."

While the celebration was joyful, the mood was solemn and somber. People were standing around in circles discussing things in hushed tones that arose my suspicions and curiosity. I was not supposed to be eavesdropping on adult conversations, but I could sense that something serious was taking place. I soon found out that the topic of great concern was Kristallnacht (Night of Broken Glass) and the persecution of Jews in Germany. Hitler's goons conducted raids killing Jews and destroying their property.

This was another sign of the rise of anti-Semitism in Germany, and the fear of it was spreading to neighboring countries. I was alarmed by it and concerned, because anti-Semitism existed in Poland, where I had felt it on a daily basis in school. It was at this point when my uncle Moses noticed me and realized that my sensitivities were shaken.

I was not like the other children playing and running around. I was not supposed to pay any attention and eavesdrop on adult conversations. Uncle Moses realized that I was visibly affected by it. He took me aside and explained to me what was happening to the Jews in Germany. He talked to me in a very adult manner, telling me that if anything should happen here

5

whereby I would be left stranded and alone, I should travel and make my way through Europe to Turkey, from there to Syria and on to Palestine where I could join my grandfather.

Uncle Moses, my father's brother.

He explained to me that it was important for the Jews to return to Zion and establish their own Homeland where they would not be persecuted. It was this conversation that opened my eyes and ignited the first spark of yearning to go to the Holy Land and join the Zionist movement. He opened my eyes to an alternative of a life of suffering insults and indignities by anti-Semites. He explained to me that it was up to us to free ourselves of the yoke of religious and anti-Semitic persecution.

I was both honored and surprised by the mature and grown-up level of this conversation. I was proud that he thought I was worthy and mature enough to be entrusted with a serious conversation of this nature even though I was only nine years old. My uncle explained to me that my younger brother's name was Ben-Zion, which meant "The Son of Zion." This was a statement expressing our family's yearning, connection and love of Zion.

Zionism as a political movement started in the last decade of the 19th century, advocating the settling of Jews in their ancestral land of Zion. It was a direct reaction to centuries of discrimination, persecution and pogroms instigated by the Catholic Church against the Jewish population of Europe.

Members of the Zionist movement and organization came primarily from the enlightened secular Jews who were upset with the discriminatory practices in Europe. The Zionist movement advocated a total renewal and adaptation of the ancient Hebrew language into a 20th century vocabulary suitable for daily use as a national language for the Land of Zion. For many centuries European Jews (a.k.a. Ashkenazi Jews) have adopted and used Yiddish as a daily language.

The Yiddish language was archaic German in origin utilizing the Hebrew alphabet in its written form. It was introduced by the Jewish Orthodox community to be used as a daily language so that the Hebrew language of the scriptures would not be desecrated in daily usage. Over the years, Jews of different European countries adopted some local words into Yiddish, enriching it with an international flavor.

I can recall that when I learned Hebrew in cheder. I was taught to read it just so that I could follow the prayers in the synagogue. Over the years, Yiddish developed a rich literature portraying life of the Jewish communities of Eastern Europe. I did not learn Yiddish until I got into the cheder school where the rabbi spoke Yiddish to explain the Hebrew Scriptures.

I was enthusiastic about the pioneering spirit of the young Jewish settlers in Palestine being able to convert arid desert land into fertile agricultural production. They literally transformed the image of the Diaspora Jew to that of a staunchly independent, creative entity capable of introducing modern 20th century technology where a feudal, primitive, archaic system of agriculture had prevailed.

They modified and modernized the Hebrew language into daily usage and a new cadre of prolific Hebrew writers and poets, such as Yehuda Halevi and Chaim Nachman Bialik, eloquently described life and existence in the newly modernized Hebrew Language.

Clouds of War. At the end of August of 1939 we came back from our summer vacation to get ready to start another school year and cheder. My parents were busy in the store selling new outfits for our client's children who had outgrown their old ones. The chestnut tree was dropping the chestnuts in the garden, the tomatoes were ready for picking. Things were as normal as one might expect. In the surrounding streets the Polish army was conducting various maneuvers while overhead German planes were dropping chocolate bars and leaflets telling the population of their peaceful intentions, assuring them not to be worried! Rumors were rampant that the chocolate was laced with poison. We were cautioned not to touch it. The Polish soldiers assured us that they "wouldn't even give up a button from their uniform to the Germans." Everything seemed to be normal. It was like the quiet before the storm. There was an uneasy feeling, a fear of what might happen to the Jews. We knew about Kristallnacht. We knew the Germans had invaded Czechoslovakia. What was next?

3   THE GERMAN INVASION OF POLAND

In the darkness of the predawn hours of Friday, September 1, 1939, we were awakened by the loud noise of explosions. We went to the windows facing the street to see what was going on. We could hear the whizzing sound of spark-like objects passing by us and hear the explosions in the distance. To us children it was a spectacle of shrieking sparks over our heads. It seemed to us like a display of fireworks.

We did not realize how dangerous and life threatening the situation was until our parents came up to the second floor where we were watching the fireworks from our bedroom windows. They explained to us how dangerous the situation was. We were instructed to stay away from the windows and ordered to quickly gather our belongings and start packing. My father told us that he ordered a horse and wagon to pick us up and take us eastward to Krakow.

Krakow was a large city with many historic sites and muse-ums of great national importance. It was divided by the Vis-tula River engulfing many of the historic sites and Royal Pal-aces. My father assured us that the Polish army would take a stand and defend these important historic sites.

We gathered and quickly packed our essential belongings and got them down to the ground level corridor waiting for the arrival of the horse-driven wagon. As soon as the wagon ar-rived, we loaded our belongings in a hurry and the four kids jumped onto the wagon while my mother and the nanny sat in the front seat. My father chose to stay behind to keep a watch-ful eye on our home and store on 11 Mickiewicza Street as well as on his father's home and print shop on #10 Rynek.

Events were so hectic that we did not know if any of his brothers or his sister Goldie were evacuating or staying in Jaworzno. We said our farewell to our father and were on our way. We were riding down on Mickiewicza Street to turn left onto Jagielonska Street, which was the main road leading to Krakow.

The traffic on Jagielonska Street going east towards Krakow was moving at a snail's pace. The road was crowded with horse-drawn civilian wagons and columns of military trucks and vehicles. Most civilians were walking on foot with heavy bundles on their shoulders, as well as horse-drawn wagons to escape the German onslaught. The military traffic, we assumed, was traveling to Krakow to take up defensive positions on the Vistula River to protect the city from the German invaders. During the daylight hours we could hear the whizzing sound of bullets and hear the sound of explosions intensifying, getting louder and closer. As the skies darkened and night fell, we could see the traces of artillery glowing in the dark skies as they whizzed by overhead. We thought of it as a display of fire works until a shell landed on top of a horse-drawn wagon and severely injured the people in it.

This was Friday night, the time to celebrate the Sabbath. We were not allowed to use any type of conveyance or travel. Our mother was looking for a place in a village, removed from the main road, where we could stay overnight and be sheltered from the fire. After numerous attempts, she was able to find some cramped overnight accommodations.

The plan was for us to stay in the village until Sunday morning and then continue on our way to Krakow. In the darkness of night we could clearly see the sparks flying and hear the thuds of explosions. We were quite frightened and exhausted by the time we settled down into a deep sleep. Upon awakening the next morning we found out that the German army had occupied Krakow.

My Mother, Baila Siegman Silberberg

There was nowhere to go but to return to Jaworzno. Because it was the Sabbath, mother decided to stay in the village until Sunday morning and then leave to return to Jaworzno. This afforded us the opportunity to walk the two-and-a-half kilometers to the main road leading to Krakow and see for ourselves what was going on. Religious Jews were allowed to walk on the Sabbath but not to use any type of mechanical conveyance. As we came closer to the main road we could hear the humming sound of German tanks and trucks loaded with soldiers. They were proud of their victory and sang, "Heute gehört uns Deutschland, morgen die ganze Welt!" (Today we own Germany, tomorrow the entire World!). We returned to the village, where everyone was shocked by the defeat and quick advance of the German army. The mood in the village was one of complete surprise and sadness that Krakow, the bastion of Polish culture and civilization, was overrun by the German troops without any meaningful resistance. The prevailing mood was reminiscent of a funeral procession whose stillness was shuttered by the sound of German soldiers singing marching songs of victory.

At the crack of dawn Sunday morning, we quickly packed our things and loaded them onto the wagon for the return trip to Jaworzno. As we entered the main road, there were numerous columns of German military vehicles going east, deeper into Poland. We were full of apprehension, wondering how our father had fared during our absence.

Our trip seemed like an eternity, but at long last, the tall chimneys of the Jaworzno coalmines appeared on the horizon. We knew we were approaching our hometown and would get to see our father soon. We were on Jagielonska Street, passing the large garage structure our family owned. This structure was used to repair the busses from our family's bus company in town, which served the routes of Krakow and Katowice. The streets were deserted; all the store windows were shuttered and closed. Our hearts started palpitating as we turned right onto Mickiewicza Street right past our school on the way to our house.

The gate to our house was locked, the store windows and door were shuttered close as well. My brother Moses David went down from the wagon taking a spare horseshoe with him and started knocking on the steel grating of the gate. After continuous pounding my father opened the window of our second floor bedroom. His face beaming with joy at seeing us back at home.

As he opened the gate for the wagon to enter, we jumped on him and hugged him with tears of joy and happiness that the family is together again. We started to inquire how things went in our absence? Why was everything so eerie and quiet? He told us that the German soldiers had been taking men (especially Jews) and were using them as hostages to make sure that none of their soldiers were harmed.

They announced in fliers distributed to the public that if any German soldier was killed or injured, they would shoot and kill ten hostages. Now we understood why everyone was behind shuttered doors afraid of being nabbed by the Germans.

The Germans gradually increased their grip on our daily lives, by issuing restrictive decrees on a daily basis. This was done by posting billboards in the town square and in town hall. They imposed a dusk-to-dawn curfew whose violators would be sentenced to death. Hostages were taken daily in Jaworzno and neighboring towns as well.

We heard the sad news that in the town of Trzebinia (a nearby town between Jaworzno and Krakow) our uncle Maniek (my father's brother) was taken hostage and shot to death because shots were fired at a German outpost. He left a wife and two children along with his printing plant with no one to attend to. The family was grief stricken by this disaster with everyone trying to find a way to help the widow manage to survive the calamity that had befallen her. In the midst of this mourning period, my father was abducted by the Germans and taken hostage.

Because of the death of uncle Maniek, the entire family was panic stricken and worried about what may happen to my father. Frantic attempts were made to find out where he was held in order to gain his freedom. Because of our family's many business connections in town, all possible connections were utilized to get my father's release. Finally, after four long painstaking days of constant contacts and a huge ransom paid through a middleman, my father was released and came home. I tried in various ways to find out how and what it had taken to gain his release, but no one would divulge any details. All I knew was that it took the pooling of funds from all branches of the family.

My Father, Solomon Silberberg, 1939

My father looked different. He had been subjected to torture and deprivation, his beard was shaven, and he refused to discuss any details of his treatment while in prison. With these experiences under our belt in the first week of the German occupation of Poland, we could not help but wonder what was in store for us next.

The answer to that question appeared in the form of new edicts announced and publicized on public bulletin boards in the second week of the occupation. They included the following discriminatory restrictive measures taken against the Jews:

1. Every Jewish-owned business was to be placed under the supervision of a German supervisor (Gauleiter) designated by the authorities.

2. The business owners were accountable to the Gauleiter for all financial transactions, such as accounts receivable, accounts payable, and inventory control.

3. No new merchandise could be obtained without prior written approval by the Gauleiter.

4. Sales records were matched to inventory on a bi-monthly basis. If a discrepancy between sales records and inventory occurred, the business owner was not given an allotment to purchase and replenish the inventory.

This practice had a choking effect on the family's income resulting in belt tightening measures.

Another edict announced by the authorities was that effective October 1, 1939, all Jews must wear the Yellow Star of David with the word "Jude" (Jew) inscribed on it, on the left breast of their outer garment. Any violation of the rules was punishable by deportation to a labor camp.

In spite of all these discriminatory decrees, life in the community had a fairly normal pace. Public school functioned as usual except for the fact that gentile classmates shunned the Jewish children inside and outside of school for fear of being identified as being too sympathetic to Jews.

This was because some of the children in school, who were descendants of German parents and belonged to the Hitler-Jugend (Hitler Youth), were very intimidating. They wore their SS uniforms to school. Even the cheder school (Hebrew school) was allowed to function.

All this changed in the Spring of 1941, when new decrees were publicized on the public bulletin boards, forbidding Jewish children to attend public school or cheder.

Along with these new decrees came the strict order forbidding Jews to assemble and worship in their synagogues.

15

New restrictive decrees were being announced every few days making life more and more difficult to manage. It was amazing to see how creative the people were in getting around these restrictions. Since Jewish worship services require a quorum of ten men, they set up a system whereby the worship services would be conducted on a rotating basis in the privacy of the homes of the worshippers.

The same system was used to make sure that the children maintained a high level of education. Public school subjects and Hebrew schools were combined. The children were taught by hired teachers in private homes of their parents, alternating homes on a weekly basis so as to not to raise suspicion of the authorities. We learned to cope with increasingly strict decrees being imposed on us, as long as we were not uprooted from our homes.

In the spring of 1942 the Nazis started to conduct raids in which they would catch young able-bodied Jewish males and send them off to "Concentration Camps." These men were used as slave laborers to enhance the Nazi war effort in various industrial plants throughout Germany where the concentration camps were located.

They were housed in prefabricated barracks consisting of 6 – 8 rooms per barrack. Each room had twelve three-tier bunks housing 36 inmates. The inmates of these concentration camps were maintained on a starvation diet consisting of 1200 – 1500 calories per day. They were assigned to hard labor on a six-days-per-week exhausting work schedule.

The inferior quality of the food combined with the hard labor caused many inmates to give up on life both emotionally and physically. This resulted in great numbers of inmates becoming weak and succumbing to sickness. An inmate who reported sick in the infirmary for more than two days and missed reporting for work, would be given a lethal injection and his body would be shipped to the crematorium for cremation. My older brother Moses David was caught by the Nazis in one of the raids and sent to the Markstadt concentration camp and from there to Buchenwald concentration camp where he died of dysentery and starvation. (This information was given to us by one of the survivors of Buchenwald after the war.)

The absence of Moses David created a big void in the family. We missed him very much and were concerned about his fate. Our parents were worried about us being caught in a Nazi raid. They instructed us to be careful not to use the paved streets when we walked to and from our schooling locations.

The clandestine system of schooling that our parents organized with friends worked well. We had to be careful whenever we walked, to make sure that our Polish neighbors did not detect our path and snitch on us to the Germans. At this time we were fully aware of what was going on in Oswiecim (Auschwitz). Auschwitz, which is about 15 miles from Jaworzno, was originally built as a Polish officers military compound that the Nazis converted to a concentration camp. Brzezinka (Birkenau), near Auschwitz, was designed and built by the Nazis as a mass extermination camp. The Germans used the inmates of the Auschwitz concentration camp to build Birkenau. The Birkenau mass extermination enterprise had the most advanced German technological science.

Nazi Germany was the first nation in history to design and activate an automated mass extermination system for human beings. It had a direct railroad line going straight into the extermination factory. This was how it worked: The Nazis conducted raids in Jewish communities of many cities in occupied Europe. They assembled thousands of men women and children, forced them into sealed cattle cars with standing room only. The vents on these cars were grated with barbed wire, and they had no toilet facilities. Once the train was fully loaded, it was taken to Birkenau. As it passed the admission towers of Birkenau, it stopped at a disembarkation point, located near an enormous bathhouse.

Nazi officers with guard dogs forced the people to disembark. Those who were too weak or sick to get off the train on their own were unloaded by a special commando from the inmates of the Auschwitz concentration camp. They were ordered to leave their baggage and belongings behind because they were going to the bathhouse to be cleaned and disinfected. Once they were in the bathhouse, they were asked to surrender all their valuables and disrobe, because they were going into the showers. They were told they would receive fresh, clean clothing after their shower. The showers were connected to canisters of Cyclon B-12, a poison gas especially designed for the purpose of mass extermination of human beings. Once the showers were activated, the poison was released, and people died en mass. When the shrieking, crying sound of the dying corpses stopped, the Sonderkommando (special commando) from the Auschwitz concentration camp was called in to haul the corpses into huge crematoriums where the corpses were cremated and the ashes were buried in the soil behind the crematorium.

At this stage of the war, our parents did not hide the truth from us. They made sure that we were aware of what was going on so that we would exercise extreme caution whenever we left the house. I felt responsible, because it was my duty to bring my younger sister and brother to and from their places of schooling. Since the places of schooling were changing on a weekly basis, I had to find ingenious ways in which to elude German raids. During one of the German raids, I was hiding between two double sets of steel entrance doors to our house. While I slid between the left double set of doors, I left the right double set ajar and open. This allowed me to view what was taking place outside. I saw one of the neighboring Polish boys walking with the German police and pointing out the entrance to our house to them.

The Germans approached our house while the Polish boy was waiting outside to see what was going to happen. Right after the Germans passed through the double door without noticing me, I quickly ran out, grabbed some stones and hurled them at the Polish boy who was waiting to see the outcome of his betrayal and chased him away. I quickly climbed onto the dense leafy chestnut tree in our yard where I waited until the raid was over.

Being thin and wiry enabled me to fit between the double doors and to be a good runner. While this was going on, my sister and brother were hiding in a sealed-off room in the basement. I served as the lookout scout until the raid was over. The hiding place was a sealed-off room my father had constructed using the same masonry that was on the walls of the basement. He used a set of shelves with hidden hinges as an entrance door. Fortunately, the Germans did not discover the hideout. This was the pattern of life we became accustomed to: surviving the raids.

Aunt Sarah, my father's sister.

I remember clearly when one late morning I saw Aunt Sarah walking up from Jagielonska Street where she was dropped off at the bus stop from Krakow. She was dressed in a beige trench coat, her braided blond hair pulled in back of her head in a style that the Polish women used to wear. She did this in order to disguise her ethnicity. All she was carrying was a large brown handbag over her shoulder.

Her face had the expression of deep sorrow and sadness. One could sense the feelings conveyed by her facial expressions that she went through a traumatic experience. She was no longer the happy young woman whose wedding was celebrated by 108 members of our extended family in the fall of 1938.

As she came into our store on 11 Mickiwicza Street, where the family gathered to greet her, we found out what had happened to her. The Germans had liquidated the Jewish ghetto of Krakow. Her husband and child were taken on a transport to Auschwitz. We also learned from her that our aunt Rachel, her husband and two children, were taken in the same transport to Auschwitz. By this time all of us were fully aware of what was happening to these transports to Auschwitz-Birkenau. All of us burst into tears over the fate of our loved ones.

In the summer of 1942, we got the word that cattle cars loaded with Jews at the Jaworzno railroad yards were sidetracked, waiting for their turn to enter the Birkenau extermination center. It was during these layovers that my parents sent me to the rail yards with bags full of food and bottles of water. I was to throw the food and water through barbed wire windows to these panic-stricken people. At first I was afraid of the German guards accompanying the train. I threw the food from a safe distance. When I realized that my aim was not good enough from that distance, I managed to get closer, making sure that the food I threw reached the outstretched hands through the barbed wire.

As I got closer, I could also hear the agonizing cries of the people inside those wagons. It was a horrifying and painful scene to watch. I was careful to hide in the bushes so that the German guards would not detect me. I did not realize it until after the fact, that if the German guards had caught me, they would have thrown me into one of those cattle cars and I would have been on my way to the extermination camp. The evasion tactics I learned on these trips to the railroad tracks served as useful lessons on how to act in circumstances fraught with danger. It taught me how to avoid being trapped by the Germans during their ever more frequent raids. I deliberately did not tell my parents how dangerous and risky doing this mitzvah (a charitable deed) of giving food to starving people was. Knowing the risks and danger involved, they would not have allowed me to do it again.

Aside from doing a mitzvah, I got a kick out of playing a cat-and-mouse game with the German guards and outsmarting them. Watching the people in these cars and hearing their cries of desperation, smelling the odor of their excrements served as a strong warning and a lesson to me: Not ever was I to allow myself to be trapped by the Germans in any of their raids!

What was most important was that I now grasped an understanding of the difference between hope and despair. When you give in to despair, you loose hope and you give up on life. Once you do that, you have nothing to live for. It was at times like this that I remind myself of the words of uncle Moses, "Make your way to the Promised Land."

Now I had something to live for. Now the adults could no longer keep any secrets from me. I knew exactly what was going on and fully understood the gravity of the situation we were in. I was upset and insulted when my parents would try to shield me and not give me the credit that I had a keen awareness of what was going on.

They did not fully realize the depth of the anger and frustration the mitzvah visits to the railroad yards stirred in me. I finally said to my father, "Look, every year at the end of the Passover Seder (ceremonial meal), we say 'Leshana Habaa B'Jerushalayim' (Next year we will be in Jerusalem). We have been saying it ever since I can remember. If you had only picked yourself up and left with the family to Jerusalem, we would not be going through these life threatening experiences now." My father allowed me to vent my anger and replied, "Would have, should have! We are in it now, and we have to find a way to get out of it." Once I calmed down, I realized that he was right: we had to cope with the situation we were in.

I was frustrated, because I had developed enough understanding and resilience to act like an adult, and yet, I was treated like a child. I guess at twelve years of age, even in the Jewish tradition, one was still a child. The transition into manhood does not take place until the child reaches the age of thirteen

At thirteen, a Jewish boy celebrates his Bar-Mitzvah (the son of good deed) ceremony, which marks the transition to manhood.

4 JAWORZNO MUST BE JUDENFREI

All the bulletin boards in town were plastered with big plac-ards that announced: "Jaworzno must now be judenfrei." The Jewish residents of Jaworzno were ordered to vacate their homes and business within seven days. They were given a choice of joining the Jewish communities of either Chrzanow or Sosnowiec. My parents elected to go to Chrzanow, because it was the seat of the county government. The county included the towns of Jaworzno, Chrzanow and Trzebinia. Many of our relatives lived in these towns. All of these towns were a part of Galicia. (Galicia in WWI was occupied by Austria). Sos-nowiec, on the other hand, was part of Congress Poland. My parents deemed the Jewish population of Sosnowiec to be of a lower class.

The short notice of evacuation posed a problem for my father and his brothers. They were responsible for all religious arti-facts at the synagogue as well as many treasured heirlooms and jewelry that they had in their own house. These items could not be easily transported. The decision was made to hal-low out some walls in my grandfather's house and in our house, in order to hide these sacred articles and jewelry in the walls. I was allowed to witness the opening of walls and the entire operation.

The rubbish was removed and buried in the soil. The items were carefully protected and wrapped, then placed in the wall. My father made sure to restore the wall to its original appearance. My father performed the same task in our house. The job in our house was more involved because he had to work with stone masonry. He did an excellent job. When he was finished, one could never tell the difference.

Leaving Jaworzno caused enormous pain and hardship for our family. We lost the income generated by our store as well as the income from our grandfather's print shop on No. 10 Rynek. On a personal level I bemoaned the fact that I could no longer stay in touch with my school buddies. As we were loading the wagon with our belongings, we realized that it was packed to the hilt and there was no room for us. My father had to hire a horse-drawn taxi service to take us to Chrzanow, which was only 10 kilometers from Jaworzno.

My sister Ruzia got very emotional as we left the house. She started crying and shivering uncontrollably. She was worried that we would never be able to replace the comforts of our own home. She was right.

Chrzanow was crowded with an influx of Jewish families expelled from neighboring towns and villages. We could not find an apartment; we had to move in with our aunt Esther, my father's sister. She had resettled there from Trzebinia, which had been declared "judenfrei" six months earlier. Her husband was killed by the Germans in retribution for an attack on a German military convoy by the Polish resistance. The apartment had three bedrooms, and she shared it with her two children, Janek and Shlomek.

1942 - Aunt Esther, my father's sister,
with her sons Janek (left) and Shlamek (right)

Now the apartment had to accommodate five additional people, two adults and three children. We had to sleep on mattresses laid out on the floor. There was one bathroom in the apartment with running water to flush the toilet. Not like the outhouse we had in our house in Jaworzno. If I had any choice, I would have preferred to live in Jaworzno using an outhouse to living under these crowded conditions.

But choice was no longer an option. Our lives were governed by the whims and decrees of the German occupiers. One could never predict what cruel decrees they came up with next.

It never fails to amaze me how resilient and adoptable human beings can be. In Chrzanow we quickly adopted to a new routine. Aunt Esther managed to arrange for us to get schooling in the same schools her children were attending. Now I was responsible of getting four children to school and making sure that they were not caught in one of the German raids. The Germans were concentrating the Jews in one location, so that they had an easier time catching as many Jews as possible when they conducted their raids. I was not familiar with the area. In order to avoid the raids, one had to know every nook and cranny of his surroundings. I decided to spend my afternoon hours exploring the area so that I could find the best possible routes to elude the Germans during a raid.

I'm amazed at how the survival instinct hones one's senses and sharpens the antenna. You develop an ability to detect a dangerous situation and find the means to avoid getting trapped. It was a great learning curve for survival. The Germans summoned my father and ordered him to commute every day to Jaworzno and manage the store for them. He was not allowed to stay overnight in Jaworzno. Our home was now occupied by a Polish family who were collaborators with the Nazis.

My father was forced to train these people in managing the business. He taught them merchandising, inventory control, and obtaining allotments of new merchandise, which was hard, because most production of goods was diverted to the war effort. They used him for three months, after which he was forbidden to ever come back to Jaworzno or have any contact with any of his clients. My father, however, was able to maintain contact with some of his trustworthy and loyal clients. He was able to supply them with goods obtained on the black market.

The scarcity of allotments and rationing created an active and thriving black market. Goods were exchanged and traded between the Christian and Jewish communities to circumvent the rationing system instituted by the Germans. Necessity is the mother of invention. Rationing and shortages of goods created the black market. I asked my parents to give me permission to trade on the black market. I knew that our income was substantially reduced and that my father was helping aunt Esther with her expenses. I had a feeling that they would give me permission to do it. Sure enough, they did.

I changed my appearance and dressed in the styles of Polish peasant children or Polish students, all depending on where I went and what I did. My father trimmed my "peios" (side curls), gave me a hair cut, and my hair grew longer. Now I was ready to go and use public transportation in my new disguise. (Jews were not allowed to use public transportation). I had to acquire new skills and find ways whereby I could travel without being detected by the Germans or being snitched on by some Polish traitor, who would like nothing better than to hand over a Jew to the Nazis.

I had a large task ahead of me. First I had to learn the art of survival in a hostile environment. Even though I knew from my past experiences, this was a whole new undertaking. Now I had to learn the art of trading. My father gave me a lesson in supply and demand. You buy in the Christian community what the Jews need and sell it to the Jews. You buy in the Jewish community what the Christians need and sell it to the Christians.

Start out with a few basic things. The peasants on the farm need clothing, shoes and other finished goods. The Jews need food; bread, butter, eggs, milk and so on and on. You buy an item for two marks and sell it for three. Once you have done it several times, you will gain experience and know exactly what to buy and how much to charge. One more thing, you have to watch out and not be caught by the German police smuggling goods.

I was very familiar with the law of survival. I knew that once I had the goods when crossing between the two communities, I had to be careful not to be caught by the German Police. At twelve years of age, this was quite an adventurous undertaking. I have to admit that despite the dangers involved, I was thrilled with the excitement of the game I was playing. Maybe it was not even a game, it was a necessity that I turned into a game for lack of other activities I was missing.

Sosnowiec. The family and I were acclimated to life in Chrzanow. I learned to get to know the area and managed to make good trading contacts. I made enough money to support the family and help maintain it. I felt good about myself and what I was doing.

Suddenly the Germans issued a new edict forcing us to move again. The Germans declared Chrzanow to be "judenfrei" (free of Jews) and ordered all the Jews to vacate their houses and move to Sosnowiec within 5 days of this declaration. No choices were given.

My father immediately went to Sosnowiec in order to find an apartment for the family. We learned from our evacuation in Jaworzno how difficult it was to find an apartment. We had no relatives in Sosnowiec to depend on. It was crucial for my father to get there before thousands of evacuees arrived looking for accommodations. He wanted to find an apartment large enough to accommodate five children and three adults.

Before leaving, he instructed us to pack only essential belongings. He said that on his return trip he would stop in Jaworzno to hire two horse-drawn wagons for the move. (One has to pass Jaworzno when traveling from Chrzanow to Sosnowiec). He wanted to make sure that we were ready to leave when he returned. I was the oldest of the five children. I had to keep the children amused while my mother and aunt Esther did the packing.

Occasionally I was able to leave the children and help with the packing. Here the packing was a lot easier than when we left Jaworzno. In Jaworzno where our family roots dated back to the early 18th century, there was a lot of tradition and many heirlooms to part with. We had generations of history and homes our family built. Here, there was none of this baggage or emotional attachment.

My father returned and informed us that he had obtained a 3-bedroom apartment in the Jewish quarter of Sosnowiec. It was really fortunate that he got this apartment. With the influx of thousands of Jews from Chrzanow, it would have been impossible to get a decent apartment later. We beat the deadline to leave Chrzanow by a day. In the morning of the fourth day the horse-drawn wagons arrived in front of our apartment house. All of us started carrying things down the stairs to the sidewalk. Our father was loading them onto the wagons, making sure to fill every inch of space. The stuff was heaping way over the top rails of the wagons. We took everything we could possibly use, because we could not afford the skyrocketing cost of replacements in Sosnowiec.

Once the passenger wagon arrived we all climbed in and on our way we went. The trip to Sosnowiec took us through Jaworzno on Jagielonska Street past our bus repair garage and the apartment house where uncle Moses used to live. As we approached Mickiewicza Street, my curiosity got the best of me; I wanted to get off the wagon and see our house. My father scolded me, saying, "Do you want to get us all arrested and shipped to Auschwitz?" I cringed at the harsh tone in his voice and stayed put.

We shared the road with a multitude of evacuees. Some were walking on foot with large bundles on their shoulders, while others were on horse-drawn wagons. It was a sad sight, to see our people being pushed around and persecuted in this cruel way. I could not help but think, "Why didn't we go Palestine when our grandfather left?" Everyone was aware of Kristallnacht and what was going on in Germany. Should have, would have didn't not help us now!

We were approaching the outskirts of the city of Sosnowiec. The apartment houses were four and five stories tall, attached, in a row on the street with iron gates leading into them. The first thought that went through my mind was, how does one hide or escape from being caught in a German raid?

Everything was strange and new to me. We arrived at our destination; the wagons went through the gate of a four-story building into the courtyard. Our apartment was on the third floor of the building, facing the yard. My father decided to unload our belongings onto the ground in order to save waiting fees for the wagons. My mother and aunt Esther were guarding the luggage, while my father and the children were carrying whatever they could manage up the stairs to the apartment. It took us a long time getting everything to the apartment; we finished before nightfall.

I remember all of us sitting on the mattresses on the floor, sharing sandwiches that my mother and aunt Esther had prepared the night before. We were exhausted and tired; we did not even set up any of the beds or unpacked any of our things. We just fell asleep on the mattresses for the night.

Sosnowiec was totally unlike anything I had seen before. At a first glance, all I could see was people being crowded together. This would make capturing people during the raids very easy. As soon as I finished helping my father set up the bed frames and put the mattresses on them, I went outside and checked out the neighborhood. I was looking for ways and means by which I could best evade the German raids. The buildings were attached and the gates were locked.

There was no way for me to go inside to see if I could find any places to hide during a raid. There were no fields, bushes or trees where one could hide. Sosnowiec could not be compared to Jaworzno or Chrzanow. It was a city served by cable cars and busses, going all the way to the suburbs. The only problem was that Jews were not allowed to use cable cars or buses.

The majority of the residents in the area were Jewish. However, Sosnowiec was not considered a ghetto. It was not exclusively Jewish. The area was certainly crowded enough with Jews, to make them easy prey for German raids.

Groceries and vegetables in the community were limited and overpriced. In order to find fresh fruit and produce, one had to venture into the Christian suburbs. This created many hardships for the Jewish community. It also created the opportunity for me to masquerade again as a Christian boy and start trading between the Christian and Jewish communities.

Having been expropriated from our properties and sources of income, my parents had no choice. They had to allow me, even at the risk of my life, to resume trading. I had many hurdles to overcome. It took me a while to get acquainted with the routes of the cable car system and find reliable sources at competitive prices. The risk of being caught by the Nazis was high.

The penalty when caught included being held in prison and shipped to the Auschwitz extermination camp in the next available transport. To be sure, I was afraid of a number of things that could happen, but I did not dare show it to anyone. I was worried of being betrayed by some of the Polish anti-Semites who were looking to carry favor with the Nazis by handing over a Jewish smuggler to them. I was concerned that my appearance was not quite Aryan enough. I had very curly hair, which was a straight give-away in a Slavic country. There were many occasions when my heart was pounding like a drum. This was especially true when I was confronted by hostile stares of Christians traveling in the same car. Luckily, there was no German policeman around at the time.

It was amazing how my sensitivities became attuned to my surroundings. I developed a sixth sense whereby I could instantly detect a dangerous situation. This ability helped me escape many close scrapes with the law. I'm sure that suspicions were raised when fellow travelers saw me carrying large bundles. I figured that I had to make hay while the sun shined.

My father gave me lessons on supply and demand that were extremely helpful. I was dealing with a much larger population, both on the demand and supply side of the equation. I learned the ropes well and was happy with the adjustment I was able to make, from a small-town boy to the big city. I was able to serve as a model to my younger siblings and my cousins Janek and Shlomek.

While all this was going on, I still had the responsibility of taking all the children to and from the various classes they were taking.

The prohibition of schooling for Jews was strictly enforced. Because of the age differences, I had to take each child to different locations where classes were held. This made the trips more arduous and dangerous at the same time, because all these classes were held in clandestine locations.

5 THE DULAG

While walking with my cousin Janek from one of his classes, we had the misfortune of being caught by the Germans during a raid. We were taken to the "Dulag," a hold-over prison facility the Germans used to gather people for a transport to Auschwitz or other labor camps.

The normal procedure at the Dulag was that able-bodied men were sent to labor camps. The elderly, frail, women and children were sent to Auschwitz-Birkenau. Janek and I were not on speaking terms because of some childish dispute (a Brogez is the Yiddish term). Since I felt responsible for our capture and for being put in this nasty predicament, I felt guilty for not being alert enough to elude the capture. I turned to Janek and said, "Let us forget about the Brogez for now." If you insist, we will resume it later. Right now, I want us to concentrate on how we can escape and return to our family. The Dulag was located on a side street in the vicinity of the Jewish quarter. Across the street from the Dulag was a three story gray building used to keep children. The Germans did not separate the people they caught in the raid. They dropped us off in the large building, together with the men. We expected them to keep us there until they had gathered enough persons for a transport to Auschwitz-Birkenau.

The Germans allowed the prisoners to take turns to go into the courtyard for fresh air. While Janek and I were in the courtyard, I realized that it was surrounded by a tall wall with glass shards on top. The shards were made from broken bottles imbedded in concrete. In the courtyard, there were three wooden sheds abutting the tall walls. It looked like they kept chickens in these sheds. There was also a pile of wooden planks about three meters long and odd pieces of lumber with rusty nails in them that were strewn on the side of the building.

The wall was next to a residential building whose courtyard was abutting the wall. It occurred to me that if we were to attach the pieces of lumber with the rusty nails onto a wooden plank we could hoist the plank on top of the wooden shed and lean it against the wall. We would use the plank as a ladder and lay a piece of lumber over the glass shards. We would then climb up the plank, hoist ourselves over the piece of lumber that covered the glass shards and jump over to freedom. I broached a few adults with this idea and they thought it was worth trying. "We have nothing to loose," they said. We hoisted the wooden plank on top of the shed and leaned it against the wall. I was the first to try it and Janek was to be next.

As I reached the top of the plank, I realized that I was not tall enough to reach the top of the wall in order to hoist myself up. I was extremely disappointed. The only solace and satisfaction I got out of it was knowing that I helped some people escape. Janek, who was smaller than I, certainly would not have been able to make it. Fortunately, we were small enough to slip into the shed where we noticed some splits in the wall that were large enough to slip a note through to the other side.

We wrote several notes and slipped them through the wall, hoping that someone would find them and deliver them to our family. In addition to the notes, we asked the adults that had escaped over the wall to contact our family and inform them of our predicament. I was hoping that our family would be able to bribe some Germans to gain our release. But my efforts turned out to have been for naught.

After spending three nights with adult inmates in the large Dulag building, we were separated and moved into the smaller building across the street. There were many more children when we arrived. This was an ominous sign for me. I knew that we were destined to go directly to the extermination camp of Auschwitz-Birkenau.

In this gray building things got gloomier by the hour. They
kept bringing in more children, even babies, every hour. I was
fully aware of the gravity of our situation and frustrated by
my inability to do anything about it. The conditions became
more crowded as time went on. I finally had to tell my cousin
Janek that we were trapped in a dangerous situation. We were
facing certain death, unless we took a chance and escaped. We
had no contact with adults other than the SS who were bringing in truckloads of children every few hours. They fed us
regular meals, and at dinner, they informed us that we would
be taken to a special youth camp the next morning.

I told Janek that this was a lie. I told him that we had to run
for our lives at the first opportunity, even if it meant jumping
off a truck while in motion. All these babies and children who
had been brutally separated and torn from their mothers'
arms were crying and defecating all over the floor. The shrill
sound of crying children, combined with the stench of excrements, was enough to drive me out of my mind. The fact that
we were not allowed to leave the building for a breath of fresh
air made me feel like a trapped animal in a cage.

In the early morning hours of the fourth day of this caged-in
experience, the Germans fed us cereal and told us that in an
hour we would be taken to a new location where we would
have many playgrounds and schools with wonderful teachers.
I turned to Janek again and told him not to believe a word. I
asked him to promise me that he would follow me when I
make an escape. Looking through the wrought iron bars of the
windows, I saw German military trucks pull up in front of the
building.

The trucks were covered with a green canvass tarp. SS troopers with machine guns slung over their shoulder were accompanying each truck. The rear gate of the first truck was opened
and an SS guard placed a stepladder in front of it. We were
instructed to line up in rows of two at the top of the stairs
leading to the door where the trucks were waiting. We were
lined up in the corridor next to the stairwell; we could no
longer see the light from the windows. The corridor was
dimly illuminated from a lamp high up on the ceiling, which
created a very somber atmosphere.

I was amazed at how obedient the children were as they were waiting to be taken to the gas chambers. Once the doors opened, there was a ray of light penetrating the stairwell and the line started moving slowly towards the door.

As we came down the stairwell to the first floor, I could clearly see the children climbing up the stepladder at the rear of the truck. Suddenly the line stopped moving, I could see the SS guards removing the stepladder and slamming the rear gate of the truck shut closed. The engine was started, the truck left, and another truck pulled into the same position. The SS guards opened the rear gate and pulled up the stepladder in front of it, ready for the next batch of victims to be loaded onto it.

Judging by the number of children ahead of us, I figured that we were going to be loaded onto this truck. My heart was racing a mile a minute not knowing what to do. I turned to Janek saying, "We must escape before we get onto this truck." I turned to the children in front of us and told them that we were all going to be killed; they would never see their parents again. I told them that the whole story of a children's camp and playground was a lie. I asked them to start crying and make a commotion while the line kept moving.

We were at the doorway going down a few steps onto the sidewalk walking slowly towards the stepladder. When I turned to my left to see where we were, I realized that we were about fifty yards from a cross street with residential buildings. I figured that it would be a quick dash to run for it and reach safety. The SS guards were directing the children towards the truck. Janek and I were on the stepladder going up to the truck. Janek was ahead of me. He already stepped with his left foot onto the truck, while his right foot was on the last step of the ladder and I was right behind him.

Suddenly the kids at the bottom near the stepladder started crying and throwing a tantrum. As the SS guards were preoccupied trying to subdue the children, I quickly pulled Janek by the sleeve and yelled in Polish "Uciekamy" (lets run for it). I ran quickly towards the cross road as fast as I could, knowing that Janek was somewhere behind me. I had no time, nor did I have a chance, to turn around to see what was happening. I turned right at the intersection to escape from the angle of view of the SS guards, and then I ran diagonally across the street towards the gate of an apartment building. The gate was locked. I tried the gates of other buildings to no avail; they were all locked. I opened the lid of a large garbage bin that was in front of one of the buildings and climbed into it.

After I covered the lid, I took the garbage from the bottom of the bin and put it over my body so that I would not be detected in case they would open the lid. I was trembling with fear when I heard the voices of the SS all around me. My heart was beating so rapidly that I was afraid that the whole garbage bin was shaking. As the voices disappeared and my heartbeat normalized, I started worrying if Janek ever made it to safety. I was afraid to confront my parents when they question me about Janek. I did not even know where I was in the smelly darkness of the garbage can. I was crouched in that garbage bin for quite a while. Only after I heard some voices speaking Polish, did I dare lift the lid of the garbage bin to take a peek to see what was going on. I saw that the street was calm and there was no German police in the area. I felt it was safe to climb out of the garbage bin.

Once I climbed out of the bin and shook the garbage off my clothing, I tried to melt into the crowd and get rid of the smell before I could ask anyone how to get to the apartment house where we lived. It took a while before I had enough courage to approach a young couple asking them for directions. I explained to them who I was and what had happened. I asked them to lend me fifty groszy (Polish change) so that I could hop onto a cable car. They gave me the change and told me to forget it.

I asked them why was it that the gates of all the buildings were locked when I escaped from the transport. They told me that whenever the SS had a shortage of people to fill a transport, they raided the neighboring houses to fill their quota. That certainly explains why I could not get into any of the buildings during my escape. I entered into the courtyard of a building with a running water fountain. I washed my face and hands to get rid of the odor from the garbage. I went to the cable car stop and took the ride to the Jewish section.

While sitting on the bench of the cable car, I was wondering, what I was going to tell aunt Esther about Janek. Where was he? What had happened to him? I was wondering if my parents knew that I was alive? I got off the cable car around the corner from where we lived and walked slowly to our building, not knowing what to expect. I walked slowly through the gate and up the stairs to the door of our apartment. I put my ear to the door trying to listen to what was going on inside. All I heard was my little brother Benek and my cousin Shlomek playing and laughing. I slowly opened the door. As I walked in, Shlomek and Benek shouted, "Shmilek is here! Shmilek is here!"

I walked into the next room and saw the entire family sitting around Janek, listening to his story of the escape. I was excited to see Janek. We hugged each other with a warm embrace. Now it was my turn to tell the story of the escape. I yelled out to Janek, "Do you want to resume the brogez (quarrel) now?" He hugged me and started laughing. It took me a few days to recuperate from the ordeal. It was now time to get back to the normal routine. In actuality, there was nothing normal about my existence, nor was there a routine. Every time and at every turn, I had to adjust to new threats and dangers. I had mixed feelings about the events that transpired during our captivity. I found it reassuring that I was successful in orchestrating the escape with Janek. The feeling of responsibility for our capture bothered me a great deal. It taught me a lesson not to be so cocky in the future and exercise greater caution. I was glad to learn that I could act decisively and with courage when the occasion called for it. The most important lesson I learned from these experiences was: Being docile and submissive was not an option I would ever consider. As a matter of fact, I was repulsed by the submissiveness of the adult Jewish population. I wished I were old enough to join the partisans in the forest to fight the Nazis. I wished I were in Palestine with the pioneering Zionists working towards a solution of the age-old problem of Jewish persecution. I would not have been in this terrible mess to start with!

But wishful thinking did not get me anywhere except it kept my dreams alive. The reality was what it was, I had the duty and responsibility of trying to make a living and helping the family survive these difficult times. Sosnowiec was a city of contrasts. The Jewish quarter was greatly expanded by the forced influx of thousands of Jews from the surrounding towns and villages. This resulted in the Polish Christian population moving out into the expanding suburbs, which were served by cable car. The two communities were interdependent in many ways. The Jewish community provided the artisans and craftsman to convert raw material into viable products. The Christian community controlled the agriculture and raw materials to make the product. The Germans strictly prohibited any commercial contact between the two communities. This created an endless opportunity for a thriving black market and smuggling activity in which I was involved. Whenever I had acclimated to a situation, the Germans issued new orders of resettlement or deportation.

This time they issued a decree that the Jewish population of Sosnowiec must relocate to a ghetto, a residential quarter or section of town designated exclusively to Jews. The location of the ghetto was called Shrodula. Shrodula was on the outer limits of Sosnowiec, about half a mile beyond the last cable car stop serving Sosnowiec.

The forced resettlement of so many thousands of people into a tiny area forced many families to share their living quarters. In our case, in addition to aunt Esther we were joined by uncle Moses with his wife, his daughters Ruzia and Malusha, his brothers-in-law Sam and David Klapholtz and uncle Israel.

Fifteen of us were living on the bottom floor of a building, which was one floor below street level. This would normally be considered a basement apartment. The building was built on an incline with a large yard abutting the outer wall of the ghetto. This gave us an unobstructed view of the valley below all the way to the last cable car stop from Sosnowiec.

To enter the apartment from the street level, you had to go down a flight of concrete stairs into the yard. The fields between the wall and the last cable car stop were covered with weeds and overgrown bushes. It was quite clear to us that the reason for resettling the Jews into this fenced-in ghetto was to make it easier for the Nazis to conduct their raids.

The ghetto was governed by a Judenrat (a board of Jewish community elders). They picked the police force and armed them with nightsticks. They had no real authority; all they did was to rubber stamp and implement the German orders. No one was allowed to leave the ghetto without a valid pass issued by the Judenrat and stamped by the police. This was a source of income for the Judenrat and police. They sold passes on the black market to the highest bidder.

To avoid the exorbitant fees for passes, my uncle Israel had a good idea. He climbed over the wall of our yard with the purpose of finding the thickest and densest bushes abutting the wall. My father was waiting in the courtyard by the wall with a hammer and chisel. When uncle Israel found a spot on the wall that was covered by a dense growth of leafy bushes. He tapped on the wall so that my father could start to chisel out an opening, which was hidden on the outside. Once he broke through the wall, my father handed uncle Israel another hammer and chisel so that they could complete the job faster.

Uncle Israel slid into the yard through the hole to make sure that it was passable. They took a rusty old tool cabinet and placed it on the inside of the wall to cover the hole. This hole was a lifesaver. I used it on a daily basis for my trading expeditions without having to pay for passes.

Within the fenced-in ghetto, the black market was the only commerce in town. Jankel, the shoemaker, needed leather to fix soles on the shoes of his clients. Simon, the tailor, needed textile goods to make suits and dresses; mothers needed milk and cereal for their babies. Folks outside the ghetto needed finished goods produced in the ghetto. This created a lively trading market between the two communities.

I would exit through the hole at dawn dressed as a Polish student. I carried a bag full of pants and shoes, which I sold on the black market in Sosnowiec. From the proceeds of the sale I would buy a whole array of food products and whiskey to bring back to the black market in the ghetto.

The German police and the SS never entered the ghetto except when they conducted raids, which they now did with increasing frequency. My Bar Mitzvah was only a month away and I did not even get a chance to study for it. In Jewish tradition, at 13 years of age, a boy makes the transition to manhood. This is a cause for celebration.

The financial needs of our family took precedence over anything else. I was busy with the trading and smuggling activities from dawn to dusk. I had to make hay while the sun was shining. We never knew when the Germans were going to spring another surprise on us. My father was tutoring me at night to recite a portion of the Torah, the five books of Moses, which I had to read during a Monday morning prayer session. The Torah is divided into 52 weekly sections, which are read in succession every Saturday at the synagogue. Orthodox Jews read portions of those sections on Mondays and Thursdays.

My Bar Mitzvah was celebrated without fanfare. I was greeted and congratulated by the entire family when we returned from the service.

The strategic advantage of our location was very significant. From the steps leading down to our backyard we had an unobstructed view of the valley and the entrance gate to the ghetto. We could see the traffic entering the gate. Whenever we noticed a convoy of German military vehicles, we knew they were going to conduct a raid in the streets of the ghetto. We would lock our doors and stay in the house until the raid was over.

This time the Germans used a new tactic. When they did not manage to catch enough people in the streets, they broke into the densely occupied apartments at random, to catch as many people as needed to fill their quota. This posed an enormous problem for us for which we did not have an immediate solution.

My uncle Moses, who had many contacts outside the ghetto with the Polish community, got in touch with a lady named

Pani Chichowa (Ms. Chichowa), who had a residence on the outskirts of Sosnowiec. She offered to hide a number of Jews in the basement of her residence.

It was decided that aunt Sarah, who looked like an Aryan, little three-year-old Malusha, and uncle Israel would hide in her residence. If things worked out well, other members of the family could join them later.

My cousin Malusha, Uncle Moses's daughter. 1942

In order to protect the rest of the family from being caught in the raids, it was decided to create a hideout by sealing off a section of the apartment with masonry walls with a hidden entrance. My father, who had done a great job of hiding family heirlooms in masonry walls in Jaworzno, was in charge of the project. He enclosed an entire section with masonry walls leaving a three-foot by three-foot opening to serve as a hidden entrance. He built 3-tiered wooden bunks on three walls of the hideout.

He built a ceramic tile kitchen stove with a baking compartment abutting the opening of the wall. The hinged door of the baking compartment was used as a means to slide into the hide out. We had a few practice runs to familiarize ourselves with the procedure. Everything worked like clockwork. When looking at the stove against the wall, one would never suspect that it was not real. This hideout saved us on numerous occasions during Nazi raids.

I was proud of my contribution to the project. Most of the building materials to build the stove were purchased by me on the black market outside the ghetto. These materials were very heavy, requiring many dangerous trips.

The German police became more vigilant and increased their foot patrol on the outside perimeter of the ghetto to stop the smuggling activities. This dampened my activities to some extent and increased the risk of being caught.

I was lucky not to be caught for a long time until my luck ran out. A German policeman patrolling the perimeter of the ghetto spotted me. I was carrying a bag full of food and whiskey to be sold in the ghetto. All of a sudden I heard him yelling to me, "Halt! Halt!" (Stop! Stop!).

Instead of stopping, I ran as fast as I could towards the ghetto wall. While running, I pulled out a bottle of brandy from the bag and dropped it gently in the path of his pursuit. Sure enough, he stopped to pick it up and check its contents. While he was busy checking out the schnapps, I was able to run to the dense bushes abutting the wall and slide into our yard.

It so happened that some of my relatives were watching the pursuit from the top of the concrete stairs and saw everything. They gave me compliments and congratulated me for being alert enough to drop the bottle of schnapps to distract the policeman. This bought me the time needed to get to the wall. I was extremely lucky that it worked out the way it did.

Looking back with hindsight, I realized that it could have had a disastrous ending. By this time, I had many brushes with the Nazis. My instincts were honed like a well-tuned fiddle; I was quick to react to any threatening situation.

Conditions in the ghetto deteriorated and became unbearable. People had no income. Many people starved of hunger and malnutrition. The Nazis raided the ghetto on a weekly basis and shipped people off to the labor camps in Germany and to the extermination camp of Auschwitz-Birkenau.

It infuriated me to watch how meek and submissive my people were during all these ordeals. To me, the message of Samson, when he held on to the pillars of the temple filled with Philistines had a clear message for us: "Let my lot be to perish with the Philistines."

Knowing full well that we were going to be killed, why not take a few Nazis with us to the grave! I guess that being exiled for two thousand years and suffering intermittent persecutions had sapped the heroic blood out of their veins.

It is amazing that I'm referring to this phenomenon in the third person, excluding myself from them. Yes, my body is among them. My spirit and soul are entwined with the Zionist pioneers who dared to part with the history of submission and start a new life in our ancestral land.

Conditions at home took a bad turn. My sister Rachel was hospitalized with a severe inflammation in her leg. There were no medications or antibiotics to treat her gangrene-infested leg. The prognosis was that her leg had to be amputated. My parents took my younger brother Benek and me to a family meeting. They explained to us the situation Rachel was in and told us that her leg would be amputated. They told us that she would be an invalid for the rest of her life.

They asked us to commit that whatever happened to our sister in the future, we would stand by her side and support her so that she could live a dignified life. Of course we all agreed to take care of our sister. I felt extremely sad that I could not tear myself away from my responsibilities and visit her in the hospital. I was also reluctant to see her in that condition, because she was always full of life and wisdom, and it would have been heartbreaking for me to see her in that predicament.

On several occasions when I traveled to Sosnowiec, my family would give me packages of homemade food and freshly baked cakes. They asked me to deliver these packages to Pani Chichova's house, where members of our family were being sheltered.

Liquidation of Shrodula. Nothing I had seen before prepared me for what was to happen next. On this early summer morning of 1943, we observed from the top of the stairs leading to our courtyard a threatening development. Two long columns of German military vehicles staged in front of the entrance to the ghetto. Soldiers with machine guns slung over their shoulders disembarked, taking up positions all along the outside perimeter of the ghetto about fifty meters apart. They surrounded the ghetto to make sure that no one could escape.

We immediately knew that this was it! The "final solution" had reached Shrodula and there was no getting away from it. We immediately ran down the stairs headed for our hiding place, which we called the bunker. Everyone slid through the baking compartment, including some neighbors. Altogether there were 24 people, including some babies with their mothers, hiding in this tiny bunker.

There was no mechanical ventilation. The only air we had was through a three-inch pipe that was threaded from the chimney through the walls to the bunker. My father had made sure that everything was well concealed, and he instructed us to maintain total silence. There was emergency food and water in the bunker enough to last 24 hours for fourteen people. It would now have to make do for the twenty-four of us.

After a period of time in the bunker, we heard the roaring sound of heavy trucks passing the street. One could even feel the vibration of some of the vehicles as they passed on top of us. Soon afterwards, we could hear loudspeakers announcing the liquidation of the ghetto. They requested all residents to assemble in the public square with all the belongings they could carry with them. We had no way of knowing what was happening on the outside except for the vibration of the trucks and the sound of the loudspeakers, which were muffled at times.

Suddenly we heard pounding and knocking at the door of the apartment above us, followed by heavy footsteps right over our heads. We could clearly hear the Germans shouting orders to the people, ordering them to go to the public square. We thought we were safe when we heard the German footsteps moving to the exit door.

All of a sudden, one of the babies in our group started crying out loud. The mother was stricken with panic. She covered the baby's head with a pillow, smothering the baby to death. She was anxious not to reveal our hiding place to the Germans and endanger the lives of the people in it.

But it was too late. After about 5 minutes the Germans came back to the apartment above us with axes and started chopping away on the wooden floor. They kept chopping until they discovered us. The woman started crying as pieces of wood and splinters started coming down on us. The Nazis, with their dogs on a leash, shouted at us, ordering us to join the rest of the residents in the public square.

We climbed up through the broken floor to the apartment above us and went out onto the sidewalk. The women who had smothered her baby started crying hysterically, "Oh my God! I chocked my baby to death! I'm sorry! I'm sorry. I caused the bunker to be exposed!"

We tried to pacify her and tell her that the Germans had sniffing dogs with them and would have detected us anyway. It was to no avail. My parents, Benek, and the rest of the family went downstairs to gather all the belongings we thought we may need and were able to carry.

All fourteen of us, the entire family, laden with bags of clothing on our shoulders, were dragging our feet up the stairs, onto the sidewalk. It was pitifully sad to watch the way people were walking to the assembly point at the public square. There were the old and the feeble and couples with babies on their arms. All were walking in one long line resembling a funeral procession. What they didn't know was that they were marching to their own funeral. To me it was revoltingly distasteful. I wanted an uprising!

The saddest part of it all was that we too joined this procession, dragging our feet reluctantly to the public square. My mother voiced her concern about the fate of our sister Rachel in the hospital. We all knew that the Nazis would drag all the patients from the hospital straight into the gas chambers of Auschwitz-Birkenau. We just did not want to tell her that. The imminent threat for us was that we were surrounded from all sides by a tight cordon of Nazis with no possibility to escape.

The blaring noise of the loudspeakers constantly urging the people to move into the public square was irritating. The worst thing about the entire scene was that we did not know what to expect next.

As soon as we approached the public square, we witnessed a scene of utter pandemonium. All we could hear from a distance were hysterical cries of woman and children that were heart wrenching in their agonizing sound.

Uniformed SS officers with trained dogs at their side were directing us into the square. The square was sectioned off by ropes, with SS guards at the entrance of each section. We were directed to a long line waiting to pass through the selection station. As the line was gradually moving forward I could see how the selection procedure was handled.

Watching what was taking place during the selection, I understood why the sound of crying was so agonizingly heart wrenching. The Germans tore babies off their mother's breast and dumped them on the ground; they forcefully separated mothers from their children and husbands from their family. It was one hellish scene that escapes description.

As the line was moving on, we could clearly see how the people were assigned to the different sections. There was one section of only women and children. Another section with old people and invalids, and yet another section of healthy-looking young men and women next to each other. There was a roped-off subsection, which looked like an empty lot. I wondered what this was for. Upon observing what was taking place, my father decided that the family should split up. He decided that I should stay with him to the extend possible, and Benek should stay with my mother. We were fully aware that once we were separated, we might never see one another again.

We tearfully hugged and kissed, wishing the best for us. The atmosphere and tension all around us was so thick, one could cut it with a knife. The sadness of the moment was punctuated by the agonizing cries of all the families that were being torn apart.

It was interesting to notice how in moments like this everyone was pondering to oneself, how to escape the destiny of certain death. Everyone was aware of Auschwitz-Birkenau and the gas chambers. The Germans had the liquidation of this ghetto of 35,000 Jews meticulously planned. At the end of each roped-off section, there was a line of trucks waiting for the people to be loaded and hauled off to Auschwitz. In the front and rear of each truck, there were Nazi Wehrmacht (regular army) soldiers on duty making sure that people were loaded onto the trucks quickly. In a situation like this, where the Germans were able to liquidate a ghetto of 35,000 people without a single shot fired at them in opposition, I kept asking myself again and again: what is it in the Jewish religion that perpetuates in the Jewish people a feeling of voluntary martyrdom?

For the life of me, I could not understand it, nor did I condone it. I find it totally unnatural for a people to endure humiliation, extermination, and persecution, and accept it as "the will of God." I find it reprehensible. It is morally and ethically unacceptable. There is something seriously wrong with this concept. It most assuredly works totally against my natural instincts!

Those were my thoughts and feelings while waiting in the selection line for the Nazis to decide whether I would live or die. I certainly wanted to live. While watching the selection process, I started to worry whether I would be selected to the same group as my father, because I was too young and small. I noticed that the SS guard at the point where the sections were separated would occasionally turn his back to admonish and direct people to their designated sections.

I decided that it would be best for me to move back from my father far enough to see which section he was designated for. I did this for two reasons: I did not want my father to be hindered by my presence, and I wanted to have a chance to see what group he was selected for, so that when the SS guard turned his back again, I would quickly run to join my father's group. Well, that is exactly what happened.

My father was directed to take his place in a lineup of all fit men between the ages of 18 and 50 years of age. They were lined up in a long row of five men deep. I could see by the way the Nazis were selecting the men, that this was the healthiest and most vigorous group. Now I waited for an opportunity when the SS man turned his back so that I could make a run for it. There was a couple with two children in front of me. The SS man separated the husband from his wife and two children, directing him to join the same group my father was in. One of his kids started crying and ran after his father. The SS man grabbed a hold of the child and took him back to his mother turning his back. I made a quick dash to join my father's group. I went to the rear of the group. While standing and waiting for another selection to take place, I realized that I was the smallest and youngest in the group. It dawned on me that unless I came up with some inventive idea, they would send me back to the children's section heading straight for the gas chambers of Auschwitz-Birkenau.

I looked around on the ground and the wall behind us to see if I could find anything to put under my feet to make me look taller. I was lucky to find half of a concrete block near the wall. I placed it on the ground in the rear of my father's row and I was able to stand on top of it without any noticeable difference in my height from the other men.

When the SS troopers questioned people about their occupations, they started with the front row first. I heard them ask my father, "Haben sie einen Beruf?" (Do you have a profession?) "Ja, ich bin Maurer," my father replied. (Yes, I am a mason.). The trooper directed my father to go to the group on the left where the able-bodied and young men were standing. When he turned to me, I looked at straight into his monocles. When he asked me, "Was machst du denn?" (What do you do?), I said, "Ich bin ein Maurers Helfer." (I am an assistant mason.) He ordered me to go to the same group where my father was.

I waited a few seconds to make sure that he would not see me stepping off the concrete block, and joined my father's group with a deep sigh of relief. I was elated at having the good fortune of being with my father. I loved and respected him very much, and I wanted to be with him. I made sure not to cling to him during this entire process in order not to hurt his chances for survival. I was glad to be with him and to share our fate together.

Based on the makeup of the group we were with, we knew that we were most likely going to a labor camp. But we did not know when and where. While we had a temporary reprieve and were somewhat relieved to know that we were not going to the gas chambers of Auschwitz-Birkenau, our hearts were heavy with grief and sorrow for the plight of our families. What amazes me most is that during the time I was concentrating on the outcome of my own fate, I did not hear the sobbing and screaming of mothers being separated from their loved ones. I did not hear the babies crying when they were torn away from their mother's arms. I guess the adrenalin of self-preservation blocks everything else when a person is concentrating on saving himself.

In times like this, when you feel all this pain and listen to the agonizing cries of people pleading for help, the obvious question is: Does God hear all these cries? If he does, why doesn't he do something to help these people out of their miserable predicament? I often pondered about this! I know I did not hear when I had my own agenda; I wonder what God had on his agenda that was so important that he had to ignore all this pain and suffering. I guess you have to answer this question for yourself!

I always come back to the same question whenever I witness this vast injustice perpetrated on the Jews, and yet I fail to understand why they go to their death with the words, "Shma Israel Adonai Eloheinu Adonai Echad." (Hear O Israel. God is our God. There is only one God). What kind of paying tribute to God was this, putting your life on the line? I had this discussion with my father, who was an orthodox Jew.

I expressed my rage to him about this kind of martyrdom, but it got me nowhere. It always left me fuming with rage. I always got the answer that we cannot question God's plans. I finally said to my father, "If I am always left to my own devices and cannot expect God to help me, then why should I believe in God?" His pat answer was, "Belief in God is unquestionable. It is our tradition!"

6 THE QUEST FOR SURVIVAL

At what price is survival worth the effort? The thought entered my mind when I started wondering whether this putrid existence was worth living for. All around me I witnessed the diminution of ethical and moral values that were a beacon of Jewish teaching and traditions. The breach of those values was apparent in many aspects of life.

It started with the Judenrat, where Jewish elders agreed to be complicit in aiding the Nazis just so that they might save their lives. The same holds true for the Jewish police who were enforcing German edicts on their fellow Jews. The Jewish police were aiding the Nazis while they were perpetrating the most heinous crimes during the liquidation of the Shrodula ghetto, just so that maybe their lives would be spared. Even the Nazis had nothing but utter disdain for these people.

I now recollect a situation in my own family. The brother-in-law of my uncle Moses, Samuel Klapholtz, stooped to one of the lowest levels of human behavior. He was cooperating and conspiring with Nazi officers by traveling with them to various labor camps in Germany. In the camps he would meet with the inmates and gain their confidence. He would extract from them information about the location of the hiding places where their family jewels and valuables were buried, by promising them better food rations and other privileges plus a piece of the loot. None of the promises were kept.

They simply robbed the valuables and split them among themselves. I was ashamed that even a distant member of my family was such a low-life and behaved in a treacherous manner. As a matter of fact, I remember having a confrontation with him and calling him a "musor" in Yiddish (a traitor), for which he slapped me in the face.

I even recollect my father exchanging some harsh words with him in my defense. It is in times of such great depravity when the human being is confronted to meet the test of time. Even at these final hours, the Jewish police were doing the bidding of the Nazis.

A Jewish policeman ordered us to put all our belongings in one pile and line up to get on the trucks, which would take us to our new destination. He told us that our belongings would accompany us on a separate truck and that we would get them as soon as we arrived at our destination. We were certain that they would be pilfering through our belongings before loading them onto the truck.

The line was moving in an orderly fashion. Heavily armed Nazis with police dogs surrounded the place. It was unthinkable to escape now. First of all, I would have to have a place to escape to. I also had to think about the repercussions my escape would have on my father. You can rest assured that the Jewish police would inform the Nazis that he was my father. They would just take him out and shoot him in front of the entire group as a deterrent that no one would ever dare to escape again.

Another extremely important factor in preventing me from considering an escape was the fact that I was with my father. I went through all the maneuvering in order to be with my father. Why spoil it now. At least I thought about it enough, to come to realize that escape was unthinkable.

Walking up the platform of the truck, I turned around to see if I could spot my mother and Benek to get a last glimpse of them and wave a good bye to them. The place was crowded; the crying was so loud and intense that I could not get a chance to say my last good bye. My eyes just welled up in tears. I sat down on one of the planks on the truck that was used as a bench. My father was seated diagonally across from me. The truck had two rows of planks that were used as a bench. The prisoners were sitting back to back. Once the truck was loaded to full capacity, the back door was pulled up and the tarp was lowered in the back, leaving us in total darkness.

The engine roared and the truck inched slowly out of the public square. As the sound of the agonizing cries gradually subsided, I could hear the revving sound of the SS motorcycles escorting our truck. All I was left with now in the darkness of the truck was the last glimpse of the public square. A picture of hell on earth, where babies were torn away from their mother's breast, wives separated from their husbands, children separated from their parents.

I was thinking of my sister Rachel and wondering what her fate would be. Suddenly it felt like my head was going round and round like a carousel with pictures of all the members of my large family, wondering what had happened to them. When the carousel stopped spinning, I was wondering if the people sitting next to me felt the same pain and anguish I did. I bet they were having a much more difficult time than I did. They were much older than I was, most likely married and had children they were now separated from. Every person on this truck carried his own baggage of sorrow. What a pitiful world!

7 ANNABERG

After a two-hour journey, the truck came to a halt. The escorting SS troopers raised the tarps and lowered the gate. We were ordered to get off the truck and assemble in an open field for registration and assignment of living quarters. It was still daylight, which enabled me to take a good look at the surrounding area.

A barbed wire fence with watchtowers surrounded us fifty meters apart around the entire perimeter as far as the eye could see. The camp was located in the midst of a deep forest with a strong fragrance from the pine trees permeating the air. The entire transport of prisoners was lined up in rows of five men deep waiting to be processed. While waiting for the roll call, I looked around to check out the surrounding area to see if there was any possible way for us to escape from this trap.

The barbed wire fence with the sentry towers all around it looked foreboding. I was especially concerned when I saw the electrical implements on the cement posts of the fence. There were occasional white signs with a red skull painted on them.

High Voltage Fence.

The words "Vorsicht, Hochspannung, Lebensgefahr" (Caution, High Voltage, Danger) were printed on it. It clearly was a warning saying the fence was electric; anyone attempting to escape would be electrocuted.

There were some other major concerns nullifying the notion of an escape. For one thing, I could not consider escaping alone without my father. They would torture and then execute my father upon finding out that I escaped. The dense forest posed another problem. I was afraid that we would get lost in the forest or attacked by wild animals. It was a temporary thrill to conjure up all these possible scenarios of escape, none of them would have worked out.

I did not share my pipe dreams of escape with my father; he would have told me that I was crazy. I could not possibly change that attitude of mine. It just runs in my veins to find my way out of being trapped.

After a long wait, a group of SS troopers with German shepherd dogs on a leash appeared. They were accompanied by a group of people in blue-and-white striped uniforms with caps on their heads.

The SS commander who carried a bullhorn made an announcement, telling us that the people in the striped uniforms were fellow prisoners who had come here to help and inform us on how to conduct our lives in the camp. They were responsible for making sure that all orders were faithfully executed. We were told and warned that any attempt to escape was punishable by death. Anyone attempting to go through the barbed wire fence would be electrocuted.

The commander passed to these uniformed prisoners pads of paper and assigned them to different segments of the newly arrived transport. He instructed them to make a list of the name, occupation and age of each prisoner. He requested that the prisoners be assigned accommodation in barracks in accordance with their occupational skills. These uniformed prisoners were enforcing the orders of the Nazis. They spoke Yiddish and Polish to us, trying to gain our confidence and trust. They were known as Kapos who, for larger food rations and some other privileged physical comforts, had sold out their allegiance to the Nazis.

The Kapos had control of our daily life inside the camp from now on. The Kapos told us that we would be thoroughly cleansed before we could be assigned to our barracks. The Kapos ordered us to totally undress and surrender all our valuables. We went through a line of barbers that cut our hair to the skin, and through a head-to-toe cleansing process. Our bodies were sprayed with Lysol.

Before we could enter the showers, we were handed a bar of soap that felt like a sand bar. For a towel, we were given a linen cloth that had very little absorption capacity. Upon exiting from the shower, we were confronted by Kapos wielding night sticks rushing us to get to the assembly and line up for another roll call.

Being afraid and hurried, people grabbed whatever they could in order to avoid being hit by the Kapos. We found that the clothing had been gone through with a fine-toothed comb while we were in the showers. My father lost a treasured pocket watch, which had been an heirloom of the Silberberg family for generations. He also lost Swiss bank notes that had been sewn into the collar of his jacket.

At the roll call we were issued patches with a number assigned to each prisoner. The patches with the number were to be sewn on the left upper chest of our outer garment. Henceforth, we were addressed and identified by our number only. My father was Häftling Nummer 178508 (prisoner number 178508) and I was number 178509.

The inmates were divided into groups and assigned to rooms in the barracks. Each room consisted of two rows of seven two-tier bunks. This housed twenty-eight prisoners to a room. Between each pair of bunks there were four cubbyholes with a hinged door on each, where the prisoners could keep their personal items and rations. I shared a set of two-tier bunks with my father. My father slept on the lower bunk and I slept on the top bunk.

The washroom and toilet facilities were in the middle of the barrack on opposite sides of each other. The barrack was split in the middle by a narrow corridor from one end to the other with an exit door on each end. There were four rooms on either side of the washroom with a total of two-hundred-and-twenty-four prisoners to a barrack. The bathroom had no stalls; there were just open rows of toilets.

The washroom had two long rows with a long funnel serving as a sink. The pipe was perforated, sprinkling water through the entire length. You can picture the pandemonium that took place in these facilities every morning when we woke up and in the evening when we returned from work.

The kitchen detail finally arrived with a bucket of hot soup. A Kapo ladled out the watery fluid that they called soup and issued the daily ration of bread and margarine to each prisoner. The quality and quantity of food was hardly enough to live on and keep working. The problem was that it did not result in immediate starvation. Life just lingered on to cause a gradual deterioration of the body, resulting in an agonizing death.

While teetering between life and death, the Germans exploited us until our last breath to perform manual labor for them.

Once a week the prisoners were issued a ration of machorka (a coarse tobacco), made out of wood, pulp and sugar. Since my father and I were non-smokers, we were able to trade our tobacco ration for a four-ounce sugar ration. This was of enormous help in allowing us to sustain the rigorous workload.

The Kapo told us that the wake up call was at 7:00 a.m. All of us must be lined up at the assembly place at 7:30 a.m. for work detail. The one thing one can expect from Germans is punctuality. At exactly 7:00 a.m. the sirens went off, the Kapos with bullhorns were in every barrack rushing the prisoners to go to the assembly point for roll call.

The stampede to the toilets and washroom was terribly dangerous, as people were almost trampled to death trying to avoid being beaten by the Kapos. We made it to the roll call assembly in one piece. My father, the mason, was assigned to work on construction of new barracks in the newly dug-up areas of the camp. Fortunately I was assigned to be his assistant.

Our task was to build foundations for the erection of new barracks. We first dug the trenches for the foundation, set up the forms with steel enforcement rods. At this point, we had to wait for the inspection by a Nazi engineer, before we could pour the foundation. The Nazis never allowed us to use cement-mixing machines. They insisted that we mix everything by hand. While the freshly poured cement was curing, the Nazis made us dig trenches to prepare for the next foundation. The Kapos were constantly standing over our heads with sticks in their hand, making sure that we keep working all the time.

During the lunch break the kitchen detail, under supervision of a Kapo, came along to dole out some watery soup to the prisoners. Most prisoners wanted to be the last in the soup line so that they could get a few morsels of veggies from the bottom of the bucket. It was rare that the Kapo immersed the ladle deep enough into the bucket so that everyone received a fair share of the ingredients. He did this only for people he favored. Many times this caused pushing and shoving by the prisoners. On some occasions, fights ensued.

Annaberg was an isolated camp located in a deep forest. Because all our work consisted of construction performed inside the camp, we had no contact with the outside world. There were occasions, however, where foreign nationals (non-Germans) would be trucking in construction materials.

It was during these occasions that we were updated on what was happening on the war front. We were exuberant to hear that the Russians broke through the German lines and were advancing westward. We were excited to hear that the Allies had landed in France. The news was a morale booster for us, even though it did not change the misery we were experiencing.

The drudgery of a daily routine of hard work on a starvation diet was very hard for me to take. I was extremely troubled by the fact that we were in an isolated camp situated in a deep forest with no chance to escape.

It was not the physical aspect of hard labor and starvation diet that bothered me. It was the mental and emotional anguish of being trapped in a cage without any prospect of improvement that frustrated me. I was waking up nights in a fit of anger trying to dream and scheme my way out of this miserable confinement, only to wake up in the morning to the same routine. I was used to being creative and inventive in finding my way out of almost any uncomfortable situation. Here all I could do was complain about it. Fortunately my father was always around to lend me an ear and allowed me to blow off steam. I do not know what I would have done without him. He had this aura of a saint about him. He was able to calm me down by constantly preaching to me the importance of faith and optimism. He kept insisting that with patience, optimism, hope and perseverance we would survive this ordeal. He used to say faith, but he knew how that word irritated me. I kept telling him that faith was blind. One could not face the world with closed eyes and a closed mind.

We surely had our differences, but I loved him. Only he was able to put some sense into my head and get me to be practical about the situation. In reality, I had no choice in the matter.

Any action on my part in these circumstances would have resulted in disastrous consequences.

The construction project assigned to us was reaching completion. One must give the Nazis credit for meticulous organization and execution of the project. Each crew, from foundation to the finished roof, had their tasks well defined and delineated in an organized way. Of course, the Kapos made sure to claim credit for that. It was because of them that the job reached completion without being sabotaged and on schedule. Now they were looking to get their reward.

The rewards the Kapos received were totally out of proportion to the pain they inflicted on the prisoners. The Nazis let them have all the food they wanted, gave them a real mattress to sleep on, and warmer clothing to wear. They gave them power and free reign to treat the prisoners as they wished. Power certainly is corrupting. The Kapos used this power to serve their German masters. They would beat the prisoners whenever they failed to meet the production quota on the scheduled date. They would deny prisoners their daily food ration if they did not comply with their whims. This was a very harsh and cruel punishment, because the prisoners who were denied their rations often got sick.

A prisoner was not allowed to be sick for more than two days. If one reported sick for longer than two days, he was sent to the medical section. At the medical section, he was given a lethal injection, and the corpse was sent to the crematorium.

After four months of hard work, the project was completed. The alarms went off and the Kapos with their bullhorns ordered everyone to report for roll call at the Appellplatz (assembly place).

We were given orders to report the following morning at 7:00 a.m. at the Appellplatz. At 6:00 a.m. the sirens went off and the Kapos went with their bullhorns from barrack to barrack. The Kapos instructed all the prisoners to take all their belongings, including the tin canister and blanket, to the roll call. When we noticed a row of trucks at the gate of the camp, we knew something was up. We were told to line up and move towards the trucks. By now I was used to the process. This time it was different: there were no planks to sit on. They squeezed in as many people as they could, standing room only! The gate was closed, the tarps were pulled down, the motorcycles revved and we were on our way. It was hard rocking in a standing position in a moving truck. Luckily, the trip lasted only half an hour.

8 BLECHHAMMER

We heard music as the truck slowed down and came to a stop. The gate was lowered and the tarp was pulled up by men in blue and white uniforms. As we were getting off the truck, I saw a barbed wire double-gated fence. Next to the gate on a wooden platform, a group of musicians were playing music. The musicians were also dressed in blue and white uniforms. I thought it was very nice of them to welcome us with live music. I started thinking that this may be a welcome change and life would improve.

As we marched towards the Appellplatz (assembly place), I noticed many similarities between this camp and Annaberg. Blechhammer was located in the midst of a dense forest. It had a double barbed wire fence with watchtowers every fifty meters. The barbed wire fence was totally electrified with the same white and red signs on the ground. Everything was almost a replica of what I had seen in Annaberg except for the size.

Blechhammer was much larger than Annaberg. Another noticeable difference was that the ground between the two fences had a wire mesh with spikes spread all over it. I asked my father if he knew the significance of the wire mesh. He said that in addition to the electric fence there was a minefield between the fences to catch anyone who tried to escape during a power failure. He warned me not to even think about this as an escape route; it would be certain suicide.

The SS guards with their German shepherds, along with a contingent of Kapos, divided the transport to different work groups and assigned them to barracks. I was lucky to be assigned with my father to the same room. However, I was assigned to a different work group. We were instructed to line up in the morning with our work group commander and not with our barrack group. We were not allowed to go into our rooms until we passed through our delousing (get rid of lice) process. This was quite an ordeal. First we had to totally disrobe and go through a line to be examined by a male doctor for various diseases. The hair styling here was somewhat different. Aside from the normal hair cut, the barbers made a very close cut in the middle of the head, calling it "die Läusestraße" (street for lice). Here, again, we were issued the same sandy soap that felt like an abrasive.

The layout of the barracks with washrooms and bathrooms in the center was the same and so were the rooms. After being doused with a layer of Lysol (a disinfectant) all over our bodies, we went into a room where a Kapo told us that in this camp everyone would wear a blue-and-white striped uniform, which he handed out to us. Here we were issued the patch with our number on it, which was sewn onto our jackets by a group of tailors. Each work group had their own Kapo as a commander. He told us exactly where to report to him for the 7 o'clock roll call the next morning. We were issued new tin canisters with a striped bag for our rations. We lined up for our daily ration of bread and margarine that was issued along with the watery soup. The weekly ration of sugar and tobacco was issued on Saturday.

We maintained the same sleeping arrangements we had had in Annaberg. As I went into my bunk, I wondered what it was going to be like the next morning when I was not going to work with my father. At 6 a.m. sharp, I woke up from the shrilling sound of sirens. My father was standing at the side of the bunks saying his morning prayers.

Blechhammer Concentration Camp
Entrance and Watchtower

I jumped off the bunk to go to the latrine. The place was a mad house. There was not a toilet available, nor was there a spot available at the water funnel, where I could wash my face.

Three-tier bunks for prisoners

Everybody was pushing and shoving, trying to get to the Appellplatz (assembly place) in time for roll call. No one wanted
to antagonize the Kapo at the first meeting. I had a problem
with the striped uniform they had given me: it was much too
big. I guess they did not make them with a 14-year-old boy in
mind. It took me quite a while to fold in the bottom of my
pants and the sleeves of my jacket. I had to make many ad-

justments to this outfit to make it look half-way decent. I hugged my father and said good-bye to him as we were leaving the barracks to join different work groups at the Appell-platz.

HALT ! STOJ! - STOP!

I became anxious and scared, not knowing what to expect once I joined my work detail. Much to my surprise, when I joined the group, I had a congenial reception by my fellow prisoners. This helped alleviate my anxiety. Even the Kapo asked me, "How the hell did you get in here?" I answered, "I walked." He started laughing and said, "You are a wise guy, eh?" I left it at that. I felt good that I had broken the ice with a Kapo. We lined up in a long column in rows of five deep. The prisoners on the two outside rows were shackled together; the prisoners in the interior rows were handcuffed to each other. This made any notion of escape totally impossible. The Kapo took a head count of his work group and reported it to the SS camp commander, after which the column started marching towards the exit gates. Being shackled and handcuffed got me startled. As a matter of fact, it got me scared and upset. I could not get myself to voice my fears to the men on either side of me. I figured maybe they had the same apprehensions and misgivings about this procedure as I did.

As we approached the gate, I saw the wooden platform with the musicians playing tunes from various nations. I guess it was meant to cheer us up on the way to work. At first we had quite a problem coordinating our marching, being handcuffed and shackled. But after a while, we got the idea and managed. We were walking for quite some time on a paved road situated deep in the forest. The Kapo was in front of the work group; the sides we were guarded by armed SS troopers. Suddenly, we could see the sky along with chimneys of some industrial complex in the horizon. We later called this industrial complex the "Baustelle" (construction site). The area was fenced-in with a nine-foot steel-mesh fence and a rollaway gate.

We went through the gate and were led to a vast construction site. The shackles and handcuffs were taken off, and the prisoners were assigned to different workstations. I was assigned to a small group handling the erection of beams and connecting them together. The Kapo introduced me to a German welder, and he told me that I was going to be working as a helper to the welder. I was to faithfully obey all his instructions and pay close attention to all his advice. Herr Frank (Mr. Frank), the welder, had a slight smile on his face as the Kapo was lecturing to me. He said, "Du darfst keine Angst haben. Du darfst überhaupt die Sache nicht komplizieren. Alles ist ganz einfach." (You must not be afraid. You must not complicate matters. Everything is quite simple.). Those words were soothing and welcome. I needed reassuring, following the admonition the Kapo had given me.

Mr. Frank told me that I would learn the intricacies of electric welding as long as I paid careful attention to what he was doing. He told me not to rush into doing anything without clearing it with him first. This introduction was a pleasant surprise to me. I was not used to being treated well by a German. I was suspicious of what was beneath the surface of all this. I decided on a wait-and-see attitude and not jump to any conclusions. I wished my father were present during this introduction; he surely would grasp every nuance of the exchange between the Kapo and Mr. Frank. Mr. Frank was wearing an old German Wehrmacht (regular German Army) hat with ear-flaps. (The Wehrmacht was made up mostly of conscripts. They were not like the SS or the storm troopers).

Mr. Frank gradually introduced me to the terminology of welding. There was so much to learn. I hoped that I would not disappoint him. He warned me that I must never watch him weld without using the shielding mask. He explained to me that the intensity of the arc was so strong that one could loose his eyesight when watching it without a shielding mask. It was almost lunchtime. Mr. Frank took an hour for lunch, usually from noon to 1 p.m. The concentration camp prisoners were told to line up for lunch at 12:30 p.m. for a half-hour lunch period. I hoped that the quality of the soup would be better here, but I was disappointed. When the Kapo came with the kitchen detail, he doled out the same watery soup that was served in Annaberg. Unfortunately, the same jockeying for position ensued here to get served from the bottom of the kettle. I utilized the half-hour difference between my lunch period and Mr. Frank's customary lunch period to look around the Baustelle (working complex) and familiarize myself with the area and the people working in it.

I was surprised to find out that this industrial complex had a conglomerate of prisoners from the entire European continent working in it. There were the English prisoners of war and the French prisoners of war. Of course there also were the Russian prisoners of war. They were housed in separate camps and were guarded by the Wehrmacht. There were many young men and woman from all over Nazi-occupied Europe who were forced to come here and work for very low wages, under slave labor conditions. The Germans had mobilized all German men between the ages of 18 and 50 into their armed forces. They were fighting on two or even three fronts. In the east, there was the Russian front. In the west, there was the front with Allied forces of the U.S.A., Britain and France. In Africa, they were fighting the British as well. This mobilization created an enormous shortage of manpower needed to support a gigantic war machine. So they harnessed the youth of occupied Europe to serve as slave labor for the German Reich. (Hitler and his cronies envisioned the "Third Reich" to be the greatest achievement in human history). We, the prisoners of the concentration camp, were strictly forbidden to have any contact with civilians or prisoners of war. I was quite bewildered by the experiences of the day and could not wait to discuss them with my father. At 4:30 p.m., we had to line up to be handcuffed and shackled to return to the camp.

While walking through the deep forest, I kept thinking about the difference between the two camps. In Annaberg we were literally walled in. Here in Blechhammer, there was at least a chance for us to be in touch with civilization. Never mind the fact that we were forbidden to make contact with anyone outside, we did it anyhow! At the barracks, I finally met with my father and asked him how his day had been. He told me that he was working as a tinsmith and that he really liked what he was doing. He asked me how my day went and what happened at the Baustelle.

I told him about my introduction to Mr. Frank and that he wore an old Wehrmacht cap. I told him that Mr. Frank was a welder who was going to teach me the trade. When I told my father that Mr. Frank was limping, he asked me why he was limping. I told my father that I was hesitant to ask him why he was limping because it might be a sensitive issue for him. My father agreed; it was a good idea to wait a while. When the opportunity arose, I could ask him about it.

My father told me that in their unit they were able to speak to some English POWs who had clandestine access to a radio and were listening to the BBC all the time. He told me about the progress being made on all fronts by the Allied and Russian forces. He even gave me a brief lesson in geography to show me the progress being made on each front. He explained to me that under the Geneva Convention, the American,

French and British POWs were entitled to receive mail and packages through the Red Cross from their homeland, which was why they were so much better off than we were. He went on to explain that the Germans were not doing this out of the goodness of their heart. The Allies had many German prisoners of war as well, and they want them to be treated in accordance with the laws of the Geneva Convention.

Our conversation was interrupted by the sound of the bullhorn ordering us to line up for the evening ration. The pushing and maneuvering to be at the end of the line went on as usual. It was a constant pattern of behavior by the prisoners. I was amazed to notice that my father never participated in the pushing and shoving that took place on the soup and ration lines. He always maintained this calm, dignified manner about him. This prompted me to ask him why he was so passive or nonchalant about events that were taking place around us? Why did he accept everything with such equanimity? There obviously was a significant difference between the way he reacted to events and the way most other people did, myself included. He turned to me in a calm way and said, "You must learn to accept the things you cannot change. Once you do that, you can channel your energy to change the things that really matter to you."

I thought about what he said for quite some time, and in principle it made a lot of sense to me. The reality, however, was quite different. Here I was, fourteen years of age, being shackled and handcuffed every day going to and from work. I was surviving on a starvation diet of less than 1500 calories a day. I was constantly seeing people being emaciated to a point where they became a "Muselmann" (a prisoner who had become so emaciated that one could see his rib bones through the stretched skin of his skeletal body). These prisoners would become ill to a point where they could not perform any physical labor or report for work. Once that happened, they were sent to the infirmary, where they were put to death and then cremated. With this reality, I had the right to be infuriated. What meaning was there to life when all I had to do was work for the Nazis for as long as my strength lasted and wind up dying like a Muselmann? I went through my tantrum and then quieted down a bit; my heartbeat normalized. It was then that my father went on to explain to me the difference between the way he reacted to events happening around him and the way other people behaved and reacted. It is important to bear in mind that my father was a very religious orthodox Jew. He firmly believed and adhered to the traditions and laws of orthodox dictates, even in the most adverse of circumstances and conditions.

He prayed every morning and evening without fail. He tried to maintain the laws of Kashrut (of being kosher and eating kosher, not breaching his dietary taboos), which was difficult to do considering the starvation diet we were given by the Nazis. Being non-smokers helped us a little; we were able to trade in our tobacco rations for bread and sugar. My father kept explaining to me in simple terms the reasoning for his conduct as well as the philosophy behind it. "We cannot win a physical encounter with the Nazis under these circumstances. However, it is up to us not to allow them to reduce our behavioral patterns to their bestial levels. We are the people of the book (the people of the Bible). We were given a higher standard of morals and behavior to live up to! We must not violate it! By violating those standards, we give the Nazis a victory if they succeed in having us stoop to a low level of conduct and behavior."

No doubt that his argument made a lot of sense in asking me to take the high ground which was the noble thing to do. However, we lived in an ignoble environment where we were subjected to cruel treatment. I admired my father for being able to maintain this high a standard of moral and ethical behavior under such trying conditions. I could not possibly practice and adopt that kind of standard for myself. First of all I could not accept the belief that God's will entailed visiting such calamity on his people. I do not believe in turning a cheek when confronted with aggressive behavior.

While our views differed on many major issues, I loved him and respected his tenacity to stick to his principals. I especially liked the idea of accepting the things I could not change. I tried very hard to adopt it into practice in my daily life. It really was beneficial in freeing me from being preoccupied with the burdens of my present situation. It opened the scope of my vision, enabling hope to brighten my horizon. It was like a breath of fresh air. The only difficulty I had was not being able to adopt it as a steady practice in my daily life. I was glad that my father was there for me to impart his wisdom and guidance.

But it was easier said than done. It was not easy for me to accept being shackled and handcuffed every day and think of it as something I could not change. My entire being was about making deliberate choices to make a change for the better. For me to stymie that urge in me would be like cutting off a sapling from its roots. I thrived on being creative in effecting the necessary changes to improve our lives. It had become an integral part of me. It would be incomprehensible for me to change that aspect of my life.

It was up to me to decide how and when to incorporate the lessons of my father into my life. In essence, the "Baustelle" of Blechhammer was a microcosm of enslaved Nazi-occupied Europe. In addition to the enslaved European civilians, there were the POWs of Russia, America, England and France. All of these people were united in hatred of their masters, the Nazis. These prisoners were able to communicate and had access to accurate news directly from overseas broadcasts that were clandestinely recorded, and they shared that information with us on a daily basis. The news we received from them was encouraging. Tremendous advances were being made on all fronts to defeat the Nazis. There was reason for us to hope that we may live to see freedom again. Hope was the ingredient so ardently needed for us to survive the painful experiences of the moment. The Blechhammer concentration camp had 4,800 prisoners, many of whom were Muselmänner, ready to go to the infirmary and get injected with cyanide to put them out of their misery. For them hope came too late.

While hope did not alleviate the pangs of hunger and malnutrition, it did lift our spirits to help us overcome it. I was fortunate to have a German supervisor who was lenient and understanding. He treated me well. I was wondering why he was so much different from the other Germans I came in contact with. Finally, when I noticed him limping again, I gathered enough courage to ask him why he was limping? He told me that he had been mobilized into service with the Wehrmacht and was sent to the Russian front, where he was injured during the battle of Stalingrad. He was fortunate to be removed from the front lines and taken to a military hospital in Germany. He was treated for his wounds in the hospital and had received physical therapy for six months before he was finally released into civilian life. He made it quite apparent that he was in total disagreement with the policies and conduct of the Nazi regime.

In spite of this conversation, I felt it was too soon for me to trust him. I had such a contempt and suspicion of all Germans that I felt I needed more time before I could have complete trust in him. Unlike the foreign nationals and the POWs, the concentration camp prisoners were treated harshly and were subjected to more discriminatory restrictions. We were not allowed to use the same toilet facilities as the civilian labor force. We were not allowed to take cover in a bomb shelter when air raid sirens went off. So we watched the planes fly over us with great joy and satisfaction. On one occasion, the shelter took a direct hit, and everyone in the shelter was killed. We were asked to dig out the ruins and remove the bodies. I must admit that we were thankful for not having been allowed to take shelter in this bunker when the sirens sounded the alarm. We reveled in glee that God took revenge on those bastards for not allowing us to take shelter.

The rule of punishment for a prisoner escape was that the Nazis would randomly execute ten prisoners for every prisoner that escaped. The exception was that if a prisoner was absent or missing in the aftermath of a bombardment, it was presumed that he was killed during the bombardment and was buried in the rubble. In this case, no punishment would result for missing prisoners. This of course immediately sparked an idea in me. The next time a siren would sound, I could make an escape and there would be no repercussions to my fellow prisoners, my conscience would be clear, and I would be free. I relished the idea so much that I planned to execute it the next time the sirens went off. What amazed me most when the idea entered my mind was that I didn't consider the fact that I would be leaving my father stranded to suffer in this miserable concentration camp. What was even worse, I did not consider how I would survive and support myself in a hostile environment.

When the alarm sirens went off next, I took advantage of the confusion and made my way outside of the fence of the Baustelle and was now a free man! All I had to do now was wait for the planes to drop some bombs so that my conscience would be clear and no prisoners would be executed because of my escape. But the planes flew over the Baustelle without dropping any bombs. Now I was faced with a dilemma. I was outside of the fence, a free man. Do I save myself and allow ten people to be executed because of my escape, or do I return and wait for another opportunity? The answer of course was a no-brainer. I returned to my post at work without mentioning to anyone a thing about what had transpired.

When we were walking back to the camp, I had the benefit of hindsight when I was thinking about what had taken place. I was thinking about the burden of the choices I had to make and the circumstances I was in. I was happy and relieved about the choice I had made. I made the right choice and my father would have been proud of the way I handled the situation. He was always careful to maintain a high standard of moral and ethical behavior even under these difficult circumstances.

I remember one night when I was awakened hearing someone opening the door to our rations compartment trying to steal our daily ration. I started to yell and berate the man out loud, thereby awakening many of the prisoners, my father among them. My father immediately scolded me for being disrespectful and embarrassing the old man in public. He went on to explain to me that the shame and insult I had caused the old man by far exceeded the value of one day's ration. I had embarrassed and tarnished the old mans reputation forever. I was puzzled by this admonition and did not quite know what to make of it. I said to my father, "Are you telling me that it was OK for him to steal our rations, but it was not OK for me to yell at him when I caught him in the act of stealing?" "No, it was absolutely not OK for him to steal," my father said, "but this does not justify your embarrassing him in front of a room full of men you just woke up. You need to think about the consequences before you act!" I had mixed feelings about my father's admonition. I could not understand why I couldn't respond to an egregious act with the vehemence it required. I attributed all this to the difference in our age and upbringing, and I let it go at that. There was, however, one aspect of his remark that struck a cord with me. "You need to think about the consequences before you act!" It reminded me of the time when I attempted to escape when the sirens warned of an air raid. If I had thought about the consequences, I might have never attempted to escape.

I was thankful that I was able to evaluate the consequences afterwards and do the right thing. It was very rewarding to have my father around to teach me. I appreciated it very much because he was thought-provoking and wise. There are two sides to the idea of "thinking about consequences." In the environment and conditions we lived in, there were many situations where spontaneous action would make the difference between life and death. One must have honed animal instincts to survive; this was no time to think of consequences. You live or die by instinctively responding to situations. The reality was that we lived in confinement under the most grueling conditions. People were being starved to death of hunger and malnutrition. The camp authorities often force the prisoners to assemble at the "Appellplatz" (place of public assembly) after a hard day's work, to watch how they punished prisoners who violated their rules. I was once the recipient of such punishment of 25 lashes for being caught smuggling a loaf of bread into the camp. I had colorful sore buttocks for quite some time afterwards. They had us waiting, lined up, for hours listening to the rap sheet they read and executed their punishment upon the prisoners. The purpose of this public spectacle was to teach us a lesson on how to obey their rules. The worst of these public executions took place on Yom Kippur night (the night of the Jewish Day of Atonement), the most sacred of Jewish holidays, when all religious Jews fast all day to atone for their sins. The Nazis had the entire population of the camp stay on the assembly line for hours while they erected the gallows. They set the stage to punish some prisoners who had attempted to escape. By the time they completed all their preparations it was pitch dark. One could clearly see a thick rope hanging from a hook with three nooses attached to it. Floodlights from the watchtowers illuminated the entire stage with the gallows. The executioners called out the numbers of three prisoners who were led onto the stage. The camp commander then called out each prisoner by his number again. He recited the accusation of "attempted escape" for each prisoner as they were being blindfolded. He reaffirmed the sentence of death by hanging, the prisoner was helped to stand on top of the bench and the noose was put around his neck. This process was repeated for each prisoner until all three prisoners were standing on the bench silhouetted by the light of the projectors.

The camp commander addressed the 4,800 prisoners who were standing for hours to witness this cruel spectacle: "If any one of you attempts to escape, you will end up on the gallows." The bench was pulled from under the feet of the victims. The bodies were dangling and shaking from side to side, the two outside bodies were slamming against the middle one. It was a gruesome sight to watch. Suddenly the rope broke loose and the victims fell onto the stage alive. The assembled prisoners, hoping that the Nazis would honor international law and grant these prisoners a pardon, felt a tremor of relief. International law clearly states that you cannot execute a prisoner twice for the same crime. The Nazis immediately proceeded to hang each prisoner individually from the center hook. I was really surprised that people hoped that the Nazis would honor international law. Our entire treatment was in defiance of both humane and international law. The prisoners went back to their barracks, disillusioned and brokenhearted once again. An eerie silence prevailed throughout the camp that entire night. All of us were in mourning for the victims that were hung, and we were in grief over the intolerably miserable conditions under which we lived. It was supposed to be a time of great hope based on the news we received from the British POWs.

The Russians were routing the mighty German army and pushing westward. The Allied armies were advancing on the

European front. The US navy was gaining the upper hand in fighting the Japanese. It was when all these great events were taking place that we, the concentration camp inmates, were living in great despair, wondering if we would live long enough to see the end of the war. It was extremely difficult to watch the gruesome execution of three innocent human beings and not be affected by it. Everybody in his own way was depressed and felt a sense of helpless resignation. To be part of a crowd of 4,800 people, watching their compatriots falling off the hangers noose and not storm the gallows to free them, was pitifully shameful. No one even raised his voice in protest and anger. The Kapos were effective in suppressing any movement for unity and change. There was no organized body of inmates to voice any protest. The Kapos had the final word. It was this kind of submissive behavior that made my blood boil. When my father returned to the barracks after a hard day of work and fasting, I didn't say a word to him. I just wanted him to have something to eat after this long fast. Luckily the Kapos were outside doling out the daily ration. I did not fast; I did not think that it was necessary for us to inflict more punishment on our bodies than the Germans did. Fasting would only weaken our bodies. There was no need for me to atone for sins I had not committed.

The next morning, the wake-up call came with precise German punctuality. One could really think that nothing traumatic had happened last evening. The prisoners were preoccupied with the daily routine of getting ready to report for the work line up, get shackled and handcuffed and march on to the Baustelle. The orchestra, however, did take note of yesterdays events. They played selections of sad Jewish and Gypsy tunes that were primarily played by the violin section. The chill of the early autumn air, combined with the sad music, harmonized to express the inner feelings of the prisoners as they marched to the industrial complex. It took several days for the routine to return to normal; everyone was shaken by the Yom Kippur massacre. The weather was getting colder with each passing day. The concentration camp issue of the blue-and-white striped uniforms were inadequate to protect one from the elements and the cold winter winds. I managed to obtain some warm woolen French sweaters through my contacts with the French POWs for my father and me. They came in handy in protecting us from the elements. The punishment for wearing anything other than camp-issue clothing was punishable by 25 lashes on your rear end. I certainly did not want to go through this ordeal again! We wore the sweaters concealed underneath our striped prisoner uniforms, hoping that the Germans would not detect them. The events of the Yom Kippur massacre spread all over the Baustelle to the civilian and POW population alike. Everyone was abhorred by the brutality of the hanging. Even the picking of Yom Kippur, the holiest day in the Jewish calendar, when most Jews fast, was indicative of the spiteful bestiality of the Nazis. It would be an understatement to say that they had total contempt for the feelings of the prisoners.

I had a serious conversation with my father in the aftermath of the hanging spectacle that the Nazis forced us to watch. The subject of the conversation evolved around the passivity exhibited by the prisoners while witnessing the event. Four thousand eight hundred people were standing idly by when three of their fellow prisoners were being hung. When the rope tore off the hook and the prisoners had another chance to live, none of these forty-eight hundred people came to their rescue. I would have expected to see a stampede of people running towards them in joy that their lives were saved. Yes, the Nazi guards in the watchtowers had their fingers on the trigger of the machine guns. Wouldn't it be worth a few dozen lives just to demonstrate to them that we would not tolerate that kind of degradation? Lets face it, we were all succumbing to a gradual death sentence by starvation and malnutrition. We might just as well die as heroes the way those rebellious young men and women died in the Warsaw Ghetto.

I thought my argument was valid and made some practical sense. My father thought otherwise. He started to explain that we were powerless to accomplish anything tangible by sacrificing that many people that may have a chance to survive the war. We could not overpower the Nazis who had all the weapons at their disposal. The best we could do was to have faith and pray to God that he would rescue us from this situation.

Once again I realized that my father and I were of two different minds in evaluating our reaction to indignities perpetrated on us by the Nazis. I was of the opinion that gaining dignity and respect as a people who were willing to stand up for their lives was worth the sacrifice of some lives. My father thought to achieve the same ends through prayer. I had great respect for his optimism. I could not possibly validate it on religious grounds. Optimism as a hope-enhancing medium could easily be validated in every day human life without any religious ingredient. I turned to my father and asked him, "Is it really necessary to be religious to be an optimist? Can't one be an optimist without being religious?" My father replied to this question with the story of two flies: "Two flies fell into cream, one was an optimist the other was a pessimist. The pessimist lost all hope and had no faith in God or himself; he just let go of his wings and drowned in the cream. The optimist had a lot of faith in God and himself. He kept flapping his wings and legs back and forth until he made butter out of the cream and got out!" This story my father drilled into me time and time again until he almost convinced me that he was right, except for one thing: when you leave God out of the equation, optimism still works its wonders. It generates hope, which motivates us to persevere.

The "Baustelle" with thousands of foreign nationals harnessed into slave labor by the Germans, served as a welcome diversion for the concentration camp inmates who were subjected to constant intimidations and harassment by the Nazis and their enforcers, the Kapos. One day I was working in a trench that was covered with wooden planks with an inch of space between them that served as a passageway. People were walking over our heads back and forth. My interest suddenly arose when I saw a group of Italian girls wearing skirts walking across the planks giving us an unobstructed view of their sexy legs. Nature took its course, despite the starvation diet and malnutrition I reached puberty. That at least was a welcome sign, in whatever form it found its expression. This was not a topic I discussed with my father. Nevertheless, I was intrigued by this phenomenon and I wished that I could have discussed it with my father.

An incident occurred where a British prisoner of war with whom I spoke several times in German, grabbed me by the arm and dragged me into a latrine and attempted to sexually seduce me. It was a very awkward situation for me; I had developed a trusting relationship with him. Now he was dragging me into the latrine, forcefully ripped off my pants and attempted to seduce me. At this point I didn't care that the Nazis would punish me. I just screamed and squirmed until he finally let go of me. I was in total shock about the entire episode and at a loss as to what to do next. It was a total surprise to me, because I had a trusting relationship with this British POW. It never occurred to me that he would violate me in this fashion. I internalized the whole affair for quite some time and did not share the sordid story with anyone, certainly not with my father whose reaction I was not sure of. I needed some time to think about what happened and why it happened. After several days of deliberation about this event, I came to the conclusion that there was no point in judging the British POW harshly or being angered and morose about the whole affair. I attributed this event to the miserably desperate conditions we all find ourselves in.

I just made sure to avoid this British soldier from now on. The days were getting shorter and winter arrived with its full fury of snowstorms. As the snow accumulated on the ground, it became extremely difficult for the inmates who wore concentration camp issued shoes with wooden soles to walk and maintain their balance. The reason was that the snow tended to stick to the wooden soles. It kept accumulating as they walked, forming a ball at the bottom of their feet, causing them to wobble and loose balance. I was fortunate to get leather shoes through my contacts with a French POW for my father and me. This was helpful, allowing us to navigate through the snow-laden street. In bone chilling winter weather like this, we looked forward to the hot watered-down soup, just so we could get the chill out of our bones. My father and I were extremely fortunate to have the warm clothing that I obtained from a French POW. We wore it underneath our striped uniforms and were thankful for having it in this freezing winter weather.

At the camp, the Kapos made sure to enforce all the cruel orders issued by the Nazis with vigor. An announcement was just made over the loud speakers: Blechhammer was now declared to be a subcamp of Auschwitz. From now on, not only would we wear our prisoner number ID on our upper left chest, we would also have a tattoo of our numbers put on our left forearm. We were asked to line up outside our barracks where the tattooing would take place. My father had his number 178508 put on his forearm and I had my number 178509 put on my forearm. There was some slight bleeding during the tattooing of the numbers, but it was not too painful. Now we were stamped like cattle so that we could easily be identified in case we escaped.

I have devoted a great deal of thought to the idea of escape. The more I thought about it, the more I realized that it was not possible; it just wouldn't work. There were many reasons why it would not work. I did not have any civilian clothing in order for me to disguise my identity; I had nowhere to go where I could be hidden from the Gestapo (German Secret Police). The entire adventure was fraught with severe consequences not only for me but for my father as well. It might even affect some other people, depending on the whims of the Nazis. I realized that this process of deliberation and thinking was a direct result of my father drilling into me: Think before you act! It was a painful process for me to adopt, especially under these conditions.

Growing up under these conditions made it confusing for me to decide which way to go. There were all these conflicting ideas and thoughts that entered my mind. At last I made up my mind: as long as my actions and impulsive behavior would not affect people other than myself, I was at liberty to exercise my judgment and do whatever I want. The minute my decisions would affect others, it was my obligation to apply honest and ethical judgment in consideration of the people that may be affected by my actions.

While these earth-shaking evaluations were not a part of a normal 14-year-old's upbringing, these times were anything but normal. I had no choice in this matter; I had to deal with life as it was dealt to me. The thought suddenly went through my mind; what would have happened if I had acted on the advice uncle Moses gave me at the age of 9 and left for Palestine at the age of 10. I would have been going to school, getting a normal education, and would not have been subjected to this terrible catastrophe that has befallen European Jewry. This was another of those wishful ideas of what if, or would have and should have happened. I had to "be in the present" and survive the war and then make my way to the "Promised Land." Being in the present meant being shackled and handcuffed, marching back and forth from the camp to the industrial complex, lining up for food rations, being constantly harassed by the Kapos and being an assistant to the master welder. Isn't that something a 14-year-old could look forward to?

Yes, you can bet it was boring and monotonous. The only thing that broke up the monotony was the frequent sounds of air raid sirens. We were hoping to see the planes dropping bombs on the complex. Most of the time they just flew over us without dropping any bombs. The air raids served as a reprieve from work, giving us a chance to get together with the POWs and exchanging views on the progress of the war.

The freezing winter conditions played havoc with the health of the concentration camp inmates who were not fortunate enough to secure some warm clothing. An outbreak of influenza and pneumonia spread throughout the camp. Most prisoners were physically emaciated and had no strength to fight it. They just went to the infirmary where they were injected with poison and put out of their misery. The crematorium was now active around the clock. The smoke of burning human flesh permeated the air.

It served as a glum reminder of where we may all wind up. In spite of the prevailing problems in the camp, there was a glimmer of hope for those of us who would be able to survive long enough to see the end of the war. We were all heartened by the progress the Allied forces were making on all fronts. My father kept saying, "All you need is faith and hope."

I was not that optimistic at all. I told him: "Hope is the mother of fools," to which he replied, "Isn't it better to be a fool and survive than a pessimist and die?" He insisted that you had to give yourself an edge in life and keep hoping for the best. Good things were going to happen to you.

Cremation oven at Blechhammer concentration camp.

What happened next made me think my father was a prognosticator.

The next day, as we were walking shackled from the Baustelle back to the camp, I saw from a distance the outline of a woman who was walking on the side of the road in the same direction we were walking. As we got closer to the woman, I recognized the coat the woman was wearing as being the same as my mother's. As we passed her, I had a chance to look at her face. I immediately recognized her and was convinced it was my mother! I poked the inmate to my right with the elbow (our hands were cuffed) and told him excitedly that this woman was my mother. He turned to me and told me to keep quiet so as not to reveal her identity to the guards and jeopardize her life.

My heart was pounding like a drum. I could not wait to get to the barracks and tell my father. When my father arrived he motioned to me to follow him outside so that we could discuss this matter in private. He informed me that my mother somehow had been able to slip in a note with an address in his contingent as they were walking by her. We just couldn't believe that she was able to do it without being noticed and caught by the guards.

The fact was that she did it. The entire camp was abuzz about this brave woman trying to make contact with her husband. The Kapos got wind of it and feared that my father may attempt to escape. They did not turn him in but did not allow him to go to the Baustelle the next morning. Instead, they assigned him to camp duty in order to assure that he would not attempt to escape. Everyone was concerned about the consequences to other inmates in case my father attempted to escape.

They did, however, not know my father. He would never jeopardize the lives of others to save his own. Fortunately the storm blew over without the Nazis finding out about it. When things calmed down, my father and I wanted to figure out a way of staying in contact with her. The main concern in establishing a contact would be to assure that her identity was not betrayed. Her new name was Barbara Siegmund, whereas her maiden name was Baila Siegman. Barbara Siegmund was a typical German name she had adopted, because it was similar to her maiden name. She spoke fluent German. My father explored various scenarios with his civilian contacts as well as the contacts of some of his acquaintances at the Baustelle to see if he could find a reliable person to be trusted with maintaining contact with my mother.

It was a complicated situation, because we were reluctant to reveal my mother's identity and whereabouts to strangers. We were afraid and concerned about her safety. We were afraid to work through third-party intermediaries. We knew from her that she worked as an Aryan woman in a Catholic convent. It was possible for Jewish women to disguise and assume a false identity. It was a lot more difficult for a Jewish male to change his identity, because of the practice of circumcision in the Jewish religion. None of the Christians in Europe circumcise their male babies. Whenever the Germans caught a male suspect with false identity papers, they would have him pull his pants down to check if he was Jewish.

The search for a trustworthy person to maintain contact between my mother and us went on for quite a while without success. I finally asked my father if I could ask my boss, Mr. Frank, to stay in contact with my mother for us. My father knew from the conversations I had with him that Mr. Frank objected to the Nazi regime. If he would accept doing this for us, it would be a perfect solution. My father said he needed to give the idea some thought.

After several days, my father said that after giving my idea some thought and deliberation, he thought it might work. The question now was how to approach Mr. Frank? My father insisted that I needed to be coached on how to approach Mr. Frank. My father came up with a suggestion that I approach Mr. Frank with a hypothetical situation. "If I suddenly discovered that an aunt of mine were working on falsified Aryan identity papers in Gleiwitz (a town in the vicinity of my mother's location), would he be willing to contact her and tell her that we were alive?"

It sounded like a good idea, certainly worth trying. Depending upon his response, we would decide how to handle the situation. I felt very comfortable with Mr. Frank who frequently expressed his criticism of the Nazi regime. It was one thing to be vocal about something, but it was quite a leap of faith to entrust my mother's welfare to him. It was now up to me to keep the ball rolling. It was one of the toughest tasks I had to handle. I wanted to make 100% sure that I was doing it right.

I asked Mr. Frank innocently, "If I suddenly found out that an aunt of mine was working for a German farmer near Gleiwitz, would you help me keep in contact with her?" "Sure!" he answered without hesitation, "I would be delighted to do that for you." I was very pleased with his answer and thanked him for being so kind and generous. I gave my father a verbatim report on what had transpired. I explained to my father that the entire conversation with Mr. Frank was very spontaneous and natural. Most of all, it was very believable.

Well, my father decided to entrust Mr. Frank with the mission. It was now up to me when and how to break it to him. A heavy burden was lifted off my shoulders. Yet, I was still wondering deep down in my heart, what if my judgment was impaired by me being so close to him and trusting all his pronouncements? I finally said to myself, "You either trust your gut feelings and go with it, or else look for another way to solve this problem." My father and I were fully aware that being able to stay in contact with my mother would greatly improve our chances to keep alive and survive the war. It certainly raised our hope for survival! My father was quick to point out to me: "Let this be a lesson to you. Never loose hope."

The following week, I took the opportunity to speak to Mr. Frank and told him the entire story. I told him about my mother walking in the snow and slipping her address to my father's contingent. His face lit up as he grabbed me over to him, hugging me and telling me, "I will be happy to do it for you. I'll ride over there on my motorcycle and maintain contact for you and your father."

The following morning, I gave him the address and her name. He said he would travel there on Sunday, weather permitting. I laughed when I handed the address to him. It was not Gleiwitz but Neisse-Neustadt, which was about 30 kilometers east of Gleiwitz. My father and I were on pins and needles that entire weekend, anxiously looking forward to Monday when we went to work at the Baustelle.

I was amazed at the transition that took place in my outlook on life and my entire demeanor. I was now full of joy and hope, looking forward with anticipation to the end of the war. What was even more important, I was totally convinced that hope was eternal. I was now a fully pledged convert to hope. It was unbelievable how my entire outlook on life changed. Skirmishes on the soup line didn't bother me; I was even able to shrug off harassment by the Kapos. It felt as if I had been injected with a new spirit of anticipation and hope. This made me so much more aware of the plight of the rest of the inmates who were sorely lacking the element of hope or the reason for their existence. The deplorable conditions in the concentration camp were so demeaning to the human spirit that they had lost their reason for living. Once an inmate had no reason or goal to live for, everything in him and around him led to the path of self-destruction and ultimate death.

I am thankful to have learned many meaningful lessons from this experience. It took a keen sense of insight and self-analysis to be able to distance myself from a situation and make an objective assessment of where things stood. It took an extraordinary event to get me to a point where I was able to do it. I was thankful to have had that opportunity.

The feeling of elation was great. It helped us get through the weekend for the Monday morning lineup to go to the industrial complex. All my faculties were concentrated in anticipation of my meeting Mr. Frank and finding out about his meeting with my mother. Every minute of the march seemed like an hour. My mind was concocting all sorts of scenarios about their meeting, none of which made any sense.

Finally, we arrived at our workstation. I climbed up the steel girders to see Mr. Frank with the speed of a monkey. I was able to see from a distance that he saw me; he had that disarming smirk on his face saying, "Well done. Mission accomplished." He took me aside behind the welding machine so that no one could see us. He gave me a letter that my mother had written to my father, and some food. I did not know how to thank him for the good deed that he went out of his way to do. He said the pleasure was all his because he was gratified by being able to help. It was indeed an enormous favor, and I was very thankful to him. The fact that he took a risk to help us gave me food for thought. It was unfair to condemn a whole group of people for the wrongful acts of some. There are some rotten apples in every bunch. I used to generalize that all Germans were bad and that some were worse than the others. Now I had to bite my tongue. You cannot generalize and make mass accusations of people! I had to hide the food my mother had sent us and conceal it under my striped uniform from both my fellow inmates and the Nazis.

I was successful in eluding everyone. As we passed the entrance gate by the orchestra, I breathed a sigh of relief and rushed to the barracks where my father was waiting anxiously to get the news. I gave my father the letter and quickly placed the food under the mattress so that other prisoners would not notice it. My father took me outside the barracks where he could read the letter in private. The letter my mother wrote gave us a detailed description of what had taken place during the selection process in Shrodula after we were separated from her.

She described in detail the horrors that she witnessed while waiting in the selection line. She told us that our young brother Ben-Zion was torn away from her by the Nazis and sent to the gas chambers in Auschwitz-Birkenau. She had been selected by the Nazis to help assemble all the clothing and valuables left behind by the residents during the liquidation of the ghetto. While working in the ghetto, she went to the hospital to see if there was anything she could do for our sister Ruzia. She was distraught to find out that Ruzia had been sent with a transport to Auschwitz the day before.

She explained how the job of gathering clothing and valuable possessions left behind by the ghetto residents had given her the opportunity to escape and obtain papers enabling her to adopt an Aryan identity.

She expressed a desire to meet with my father in the hope of rebuilding a family. The letter was a source of encouragement and hope. It certainly gave us a reason for living and the will to survive the war. You never know what life has in store for you. As my father was reading the letter, pictures of events were running through my mind, such as the family meeting at which we all committed to take care of our sister when her leg was amputated. I saw my mother's distraught face when she found out in the hospital that Ruzia was taken to Auschwitz the day before. I saw her face and felt her agonizing pain when my brother Ben-Zion was ripped from her arms and sent with a transport to Auschwitz-Birkenau. I could see the multitude of my brethren being burned to ashes in the crematoria of Birkenau having their imprint on my mother's face.

Yet with all this pain and suffering, she was able to gather the courage and strength to deliver a note with her address into a marching column of concentration camp inmates. The audacity to express her longing to meet with my father in the hope of rebuilding a family to replace those who were exterminated. I can see her walking in the deep snow with determination and purpose "to meet my father."

She not only was a devoted wife and mother, she was a valiant woman to trek her way through deep snow and among watchful SS guards in order to find her husband. Just rewinding the reel of her treading in the deep snow gives me the shivers. This is the epic of a real "Yidishe Mame" (Jewish Mother). Those are the bittersweet aspects of life that make life worth living.

My father and I shared a moment of joy and sorrow hoping that we would live to see better days. Nothing in our immediate environment had changed. The same routine was repeating itself every day: the line-ups, shoving and pushing, the Kapos harassing the prisoners, the orchestra. Everything was the same. The only thing that was different was I.

I looked at life through a totally new prism. I was thoroughly convinced that I would survive this war and be united with my mother. This feeling alone was enough to elevate my spirit to pull me through any rough spots I may encounter. And the rough spots kept getting rougher and rougher.

Conditions in the camp deteriorated more and more. Sickness, malnutrition, frostbites, pneumonia and diarrhea reached epidemic proportions. The infirmary was running out of room, people were dying at an alarming rate. They were taken straight from the barracks to the crematorium. The stench of burning flesh was everywhere; there was no getting away from it.

In these conditions it was hard to be self-assured and not be affected by the plight of your fellow prisoners. The other aspect of our lives played itself out at the industrial complex. The only reason we were achieving the production quotas the German authorities set up for us was that they would stand over us and watch every step of ours, making sure we met their quotas.

We needed the freedom to stay in contact with the POWs and civilians that were the lifeblood of our information on the progress of the war. Air raid sirens sounded all day long. Bombardments were much more frequent now, even though the flyovers were at a ratio of 10 to 1. It was a clear sign that the Allied Air Forces ruled the skies.

The German anti-aircraft batteries were a joke. They frequently went off after the airplanes had left the area. One could clearly notice the failures of the German radar system. We were not allowed to take cover in their bunkers.

We enjoyed seeing the anti-aircraft fire being off course, or when the batteries started firing after the airplanes had left the scene. You could really notice that there was a crack in the German accuracy and discipline. We were happy to see that the Germans were not infallible. The cracks in German society were felt everywhere. They lost the feeling of superiority and engaged in conversations with the foreign workers. Loyalty to the Führer (leader) started breaking apart at the seams. Yet they never admitted knowing about or taking part in the extermination of European Jewry.

The German propaganda machine, headed by Mr. Goebbels, drilled into their heads 24/7 that the Jews were treacherous and responsible for all that was evil in the world. They fell for it hook, line and sinker. They believed it, and the majority of Germans conveniently justified the activities of the Nazis. It was convenient for them to justify it when their armies overran and enslaved all of Europe.

They never thought that there would come a day of reckoning when they would have to pay for the crimes they had committed. The sad part of it was, that the millions of lives that were lost and shattered could never be replaced. The emotional upheaval of teetering between hope and despair was much more apparent after Mr. Frank had visited my mother.

The highs and lows between hope and despair were occurring in shorter intervals. My life was swinging like a pendulum between both extremes. I could not seem to find a middle ground, no matter how hard I tried.

I turned to my father again for help and advice. All my father could tell me was, "There is absolutely nothing you can do to change the situation you are in. You must learn to accept it and cope with it as best you can. You must be aware that we are far better off than the rest of the prisoners in this camp. We know that your mother is alive, and we are staying in contact with her. We are getting food packages, which none of the other prisoners do. We are receiving letters of encouragement and love. You have all the reasons in the world to have faith and hope that you will live to see the end of the war soon. All you need is patience; a little patience goes a long way." I looked at my father stridently and asked, "How can anyone be patient when an epidemic of dysentery is killing hundreds of people all around you? People are dying all around us and there is no help in sight. How can I be patient when I'm constantly staring death in its face? I never know if it is my turn next!"

The only one who would listen to me was my father. I had neither the wisdom nor the maturity to understand the value of patience. Patience to me meant prolonging the excruciating pain and suffering. There were no viable options. You suffer and carry on the best you can, or die in resignation. I was not ready to resign and die.

I calmed down once again, being thankful that my father was around to listen to me. My father did not let up or give up on me. He kept telling me that everyone in this camp would love to trade places with me, because I was in contact with my mother, I received food packages whenever we were able to send a messenger to meet with my mother. I couldn't ask for greater material and emotional support than we were now getting from my mother. I needed to be thankful and count my blessings and concentrate on seeing the light at the end of the tunnel. Concentrate on how you can survive and live to see the end of the war, instead of being morose and depressed.

Think positive. Think of the day you will be liberated and will join your mother to build a new life. Maybe your older brother Moses David will survive the war and join us. You will be able to fulfill your dream and join the Zionist pioneers in the Promised Land. Wouldn't that be something to look forward to? Just remember, if you were dead, you could not do any of these things.

My father knew exactly what buttons to press in order to change my mood and attitude. It worked once again to get me grounded and appreciate that he was around to pick me up when I was down and out. I felt uncomfortable asking Mr. Frank to go to my mother that often. I discussed this problem with my father and we decided that he would try to get some contacts through some people he knew in his work group. We decided that it would be wise to have more than one contact person to maintain the liaison between my mother and us.

There were a number of drawbacks in getting people from the concentration camp involved as middleman to contact my mother. For one thing, the more people that were involved in it, the greater the risk of exposure. Another problem was that with the involvement of fellow prisoners, we would have to share all the food packages with them. We considered all options and decided that half a loaf was better than none. We were happy with the arrangement; it seemed to be working out quite well. I was now in a much more positive mood, hoping to see the end of the war soon.

This hope was intensified by the fact that the Allied Forces were now fighting the war on German soil. The Russian army was at the gates of Breslau, and General Eisenhower (American General) and General Montgomery (of Britain) were advancing on two fronts from the West. It was November of 1944 and the POWs at the industrial complex were jubilant about the progress of the war. We were getting daily updates from them. The speed of the advances was amazing. At the industrial complex, the air raid sirens blasted constantly.

We no longer saw American bombers dropping the bombs. Now it was Russian bombers, escorted by Russian fighter planes, dropping the bombs, while the fighter planes were diving to attack the anti-aircraft batteries. There wasn't a single German plane in the air. It looked like the German air force had been decimated. The occasional snowflakes had not been sticking to the ground yet. It had gotten cold enough for people to catch colds and be stricken with pneumonia in their weakened condition. This was a bad time to be cremated, just as there was hope that the war was going to come to an end.

Despite the flu epidemic and the resulting death toll, the overall air of optimism prevailed throughout the camp. Even at the industrial complex, all the POWs and the civilian slave laborers were making pronouncements that this would be their last Christmas and New Year's in captivity.

The mood of the concentration camp prisoners was much more subdued. While we were looking forward to the war's end, we did not know what to expect in a homecoming once we were liberated. We knew of the atrocities the Nazis had perpetrated throughout the occupied countries of Europe and the mass extermination of European Jewry. What we did not know was the enormity and the scope of the annihilation that took place throughout the European continent. The anxiety and weariness of what to expect once we got home weighed heavily on everyone's heart. The fearful feeling of the un-known was now augmented by the sounding thuds of artil-lery fire we heard in the distance.

We knew that Blechhammer was close to the Oder River where the Germans would most likely set up a line of defense to stem the Russian advance. We now lived in a situation where we were leaving the barbed wire gates of the camp ac-companied by the sound of the orchestra. The rest of the way to the industrial complex, we were accompanied by the sound of distant artillery fire. The reverberating sound of artillery fire was going on for several weeks. We were wondering why the Russians were not coming to liberate us. It was now past the middle of January 1945. The snow was piling up, making it difficult for the prisoners wearing wooden-soled shoes to walk. We were waiting for the Russians to come.

9   THE DEATH MARCH

The Nazi regime of the Third Reich was on the threshold of total collapse. The rapid advance of the Russian army in the East and the Allied armies in the West had taken the war into Germany. They were now fighting on the soil of the Third Reich. The Nazi leadership under the direction of Himmler decided to implement an evacuation procedure of all concentration camps that were in the path of the advancing Russian army.

The reasons for this evacuation were: 1) to vacate the camps and erase any traces of the atrocities that had been perpetrated in them, 2) to take the prisoners of the camps westward, deeper into Germany, to build defensive fortifications for the retreating German army.

The prisoners were forced to march in the midst of freezing winter conditions from dawn to dusk. They were not given any food or water during the entire duration of the march. The Nazi guards were brutal with punishing cruelty with which they treated the prisoners throughout the entire march.

The prisoners were filling their tin canisters with snow, which they were melting on their bodies and using for drinking. Many prisoners would die every day of fatigue, starvation, exhaustion, malnutrition, and dysentery, characterized by severe diarrhea. They would just collapse on the side of the road and die.

Sunday, January 21, 1945

This Sunday morning started out like any other Sunday: the prisoners were busy with their cleaning chores getting ready for another work week at the industrial complex of Blechhammer. The sounds of artillery fire and ensuing explosions were loud and clear. They raised the spirit of the prisoners, anticipating the end of the war. The stench of burning human flesh permeated the air all around us. The odor was especially felt in our barrack #15, which was abutting the wall of the crematorium.

At 10:30 a.m. a rumor started quickly spreading through the camp that we would be forced to evacuate. No one knew any details as to when or where we would be evacuated to. At about 11:00 a.m. the Kapos were running around with their bullhorns ordering all prisoners to report at the assembly place with all their belongings by 12:00 noon.

Normally an announcement of this sort would be announced by the Nazis over the loudspeaker system, followed up by Nazi guards with Kapos spurring the prisoners into action. This time there wasn't a Nazi guard in sight. When I got the word that the food storage facilities were abandoned by the Nazis, I joined the crowd and got away with a carton full of food, mostly bread and margarine, and brought it to my father into the barrack.

My father and I considered hiding in the attic of the barrack with the provisions I had stolen and wait until the war was over. We knew that joining the evacuation would only prolong our suffering. I was in favor of hiding in the attic of our barrack until the war ended. My father argued against it, saying that the Nazis would most likely dynamite the crematorium, which abutted our barrack. When that happened, we would be discovered and shot. His argument was logical and made sense. The Nazis had the Kapos issue warnings on their bullhorns that any prisoner found hiding or not reporting for the evacuation would be shot on the spot.

My father and I were discussing the possibility of the two of us hiding or escaping during the evacuation and joining my mother at the Catholic convent where she was working as an Aryan woman. We had definite advantages over the other prisoners: we had leather shoes; we had woolen sweaters and a woolen hat with earmuffs that I had obtained through my contacts with the French POWs. And we had a supply of bread and margarine that I managed to steal from the food storage area. All we had to do was hide it well enough for the Germans not to notice it. The food we had to hide from being noticed by fellow prisoners as well, because they might steal it from us. We did the best we could to conceal everything.

At about 11:45 a.m., a column of heavily armed SS vehicles loaded with officers and guards entered the camp, driving straight to the Appellplatz (assembly place). The loud speakers were blaring orders for all to assemble. They declared once again that anyone hiding or failing to report for the evacuation would be shot on the spot.

My father and I had all the provisions placed in different parts of our body and tied down with strings so that it was not noticeable. We walked over to the assembly place and lined up in rows of five deep. This time there were no shackles or handcuffs put on the prisoners. After the Kapos took the roll call, the SS camp commander addressed the prisoners on the loud speaker. He told us that this evacuation was ordered in order to secure our safety and he assured us that we were going to a safer place with better conditions.

That certainly sounded like the line they were telling women and children before they entered the showers in Birkenau. While we were listening to the commander speak, there were rows of SS guards with horse-driven sleds and dogs at their side waiting to take up their positions. In the assembled mass of 4,800 prisoners one could feel the anxiety and trepidation about the events unfolding before us. This was another instance where the fate of 4,800 people rested in the hands of these bestial Nazis.

The SS commander issued the marching orders and a vast column of prisoners in rows of five across started to march.

An SS guard on a horse-driven sled was assigned to lead the column. Thereafter the SS guards took up their positions with every 50th row of the marching column. This turned out to be one SS guard to every 250 prisoners.

The prisoners were ordered to carry their tin canisters as well as their blankets. As the column moved toward the gates of the camp, I noticed that the members of the orchestra had their blankets and tin canisters with them. They were the last to join the marching column. Then the SS would lock the gates. The prisoners looked like a motley crew with blankets over their shoulders and tin canisters hanging at their waist. The music they played was sad and somber; it reflected the mood of the prisoners.

Shouting of orders by the camp commander frequently broke the silence of the marchers. As we walked out onto the road we realized how disastrous the wooden soles were to the prisoners wearing them. When we walked to the industrial complex, we had been shackled and cuffed to each other. This helped stabilize the inmates wearing shoes with wooden soles and prevented them from wobbling. In the absence of shackles and cuffs, prisoners were wobbling with snow accumulating at the bottom of their shoes. This of course slowed down the pace of the march. The SS Guards were alternating sides every 50th row so that there were guards on the left and right side of the marching column. When the guards noticed prisoners lagging behind and slowing down the pace, they ordered their dogs to maul them in order to keep them in line, making sure that the column maintained a steady pace. There were no portable sanitary facilities provided. We were allowed to relieve ourselves on the side of the road, but we had to return to our place running if we wanted to avoid being mauled by the guards and their dogs.

These SS guards derived great pleasure and satisfaction when they witnessed their dogs mauling a prisoner. One would definitely have to be a psychopath to qualify for a job as an SS guard in a concentration camp. I was surprised to find that despite the freezing weather, we were quite warm as long as we kept walking. The longer we walked, the more people were falling by the wayside. We had no way of knowing what happened to them once they lagged way behind us.

They kept us marching on the main highway that was crowded with a mixture of traffic. There were many military convoys going in both directions. Going east towards the front lines were trucks loaded with ammunition and supplies dragging artillery pieces behind them. Going west were many empty trucks and military ambulances.

The road was full with civilian traffic, all of which was going westward to escape the Russian onslaught. This traffic consists mostly of Germans who had abandoned their homes and towns in fear of the Russians. They traveled in cars, horse-driven sleds, and most of them were heading towards the American lines of occupation.

As the sky started to get darker, we were wondering if they would continue the march into the night. We did not have to wonder for long. The column of concentration camp prisoners veered off the main highway onto a side road leading to an abandoned village. As we walked into the village, we realized that it was totally deserted. My father and I looked at each other asking, "Where on earth are they going to accommodate all these men overnight?"

Suddenly, we were being pushed from behind with a strong force. People were pushing and shoving, we did not know why. Soon the pushing and shoving turned into a shoving stampede to a set of open barn doors. People were falling and being trampled on because the SS were whipping the people into a frenzied panic to shove as many people as they could into a barn. The result was that many prisoners were trampled to death before the barn doors were closed and locked for the night. My father and I were fortunate to find a spot in the haystack where we could sit. We were packed and squeezed into the barn like a pack of sardines. All we could hear was the moaning and groaning of people who were trampled during the stampede.

As time passed, the moaning subsided. The men either died of their wounds or merely passed out from exhaustion. It was now time for my father and me to share some of the food I had taken from the warehouse. We had to do it quietly in order not to attract the attention of fellow prisoners. This was extremely difficult to do, since we were packed so closely together. We hoped that the Germans would give us some food and water to drink. But they locked us in those barns for the night and forgot all about us. It was very quiet; most prisoners fell into a deep sleep, exhausted from the long march. I attempted to start a conversation with my father about a possible escape.

It was impossible even to whisper without someone next to us hearing it. I decided to have the conversation with my father the next morning while we were walking. It was a bitter cold night, and the winds were howling through the cracks in the barn walls. Fortunately, we had the blankets to cover our bodies and conceal our food. The only advantage of being squeezed in so tightly was that the warm temperatures generated by our bodies kept us from freezing to death.

Monday, January 22, 1945

At the first light of dawn, the sirens started blasting from the German trucks ordering us out to line up for the march. As we approached the barn doors we noticed that there were corpses of people who were trampled the night before strewn all over on the outside. No one paid any attention to these corpses, just followed the orders to line up.

It was freezing outside while we were waiting for all prisoners to assemble. We were hoping to get some hot tea or soup. But nothing. No food, no water. Nothing. While waiting, my father and I decided to pack our tin canisters with snow so that we could melt it to water on our bodies. Otherwise we would die of dehydration.

The SS guards took up their positions on both sides of the column of prisoners, and the marching orders were issued. The column was winding through the village to the main highway, which was packed with many German civilians fleeing from the Russian advance.

The Germans knew that unlike the Americans, the Russians had suffered millions of losses during the German occupation of Russian territories. They knew of the atrocities and executions the German soldiers had inflicted on the Russian nation. The Germans knew very well that they had been ruthlessly cruel in how they treated the Russian population as sub-humans.

They were afraid of the revenge the Red Army would take for the massacre and degradation of millions of Russians. That is why they were running to escape from the Russian occupation.

The civilian traffic, combined with the military convoys, slowed down the pace of the march. Not to mention the fact that this was the second day the prisoners were marching without any food or water. Because the road was so heavily traveled, the snow tended not to stick to the wooden soles of the prisoners' shoes. This problem occurred only when there was a fresh snowfall.

The emaciated prisoners who had been suffering from starvation and malnutrition before the march began, were now really having trouble holding on to life. Having to exert the energy required to walk all day, the human body requires sustenance. The Germans denied the prisoners the minimal conditions required for human survival.

As a result of the exertion and lack of food, the prisoners were stricken with a variety of diseases with the following symptoms: their eyes would bulge and they would become totally incoherent; others would be stricken by dysentery and die on top of their feces. One way or the other, they would just lie down on the side of the road and freeze to death with their blanket on their shoulder and the tin canister by their side. This was why this evacuation became known as the "Death March."

I finally had a chance to talk with my father while both of us were walking. I told him that unless we took a chance and hid ourselves in the hay in the next few days, we would end up like these people on the side of the road. He agreed with me that hiding in the hay may be the only way for us to survive, and it was worth taking a chance. I took out a piece of bread and margarine from the stash I had stored in my pants and shared it with my father. We were quite warm while marching. It got to a point where the blanket that we carried impeded my ability to walk. I told my father that I would get rid of the blanket and pick one up from one of the corpses in the late afternoon when it turned a lot colder. He did not respond to my suggestion, which I interpreted as saying, do what you have to do. Don't look for my approval. I tossed my blanket aside, and it made a big difference in the ease with which I was able to walk.

My father never compromised his high ethical and moral standards, even under the most adverse of conditions. This made him the kind of man he was and this is why I respected him and looked up to him so much. I looked at my father and pointed to the people strewn on the side of the road and told him, "If I ever survive this war, I have an obligation to fulfill in the memory of these martyrs and in the honor of my uncle Moses. I have to make my way to the Promised Land and end once and for all the chain of persecution the Jews are subjected to." He looked at me with tears in his eyes and said, "From your mouth to God's ears." We hugged and I, too, was choking with tears. The love, wisdom and understanding that my father imparted to me during those critical days of our fight for survival were priceless. It gave me the impetus for living, something to cherish for the rest of my life. My father was the pillar of my strength, and I loved him deeply.

We continued walking until the sky turned dark and the marching column veered off the main highway once again to another abandoned village. This time the push to the barn was much stronger. This caused the first men who entered the barn to fall and be trampled to death by the wave of men behind them. The Nazis were merciless in the way they whipped the people in the rear to create this stampede. My father and I, as well as the rest of the prisoners, just fell on the hay in total exhaustion. We were able to stealthily grab a bite from the food I had stashed away, and then we fell into a deep sleep.

Tuesday, January 23, 1945

The sirens woke us up before dawn, and we didn't even have a chance to bury ourselves in the hay! Now it was too late. As I started to get up I realized that our stash of food was stolen. I turned to my father and asked him, "What do we do now?" His answer was, "We are in God's hand." We were rushed; there was no time for discussion, because the SS guards were yelling for us to line up. We could not possibly bury ourselves in the hay with everyone watching. We went out with the rest of the herd to line up. Luckily the snow in the canisters had melted and we were able to have a drink of water. While rushing, I did not realize that I had a few slices of bread with margarine in the back of my pants pocket. We divided it into several portions in order to keep us going. It certainly was not enough to live on, but enough to keep us from dying. That is more than anyone else had.

The column of prisoners kept walking out of the village towards the main highway and came to a sudden stop. We saw Russian planes attacking the German military columns on the highway. Civilians were running into the snow-covered fields for cover. There was total pandemonium for a while. As soon as the planes left the area, everything returned to normal and the march resumed. It was nice for a change to see Germans running for their lives. It did not change our situation in any way. The Nazi guards just got angry and nastier. But it was a morale booster nevertheless.

The column of prisoners showed visible signs of deterioration. More people elected to go to the side of the road and give up on life. They were sick and weakened by lack of food and water. They just lost all hope of being able to make it through to the end of the war. The column of prisoners was now forced to move to the side of the road and stop their march with greater frequency. While we stopped walking, we were able to see the German military trucks driving by, loaded with teenage soldiers on their way to defend their Fatherland. The masters of the world were now mobilizing the Hitler-Jugend (Hitler Youth) into the front lines to make a last stand. While we were waiting for the convoys to pass, we finished drinking the water in the canisters and repacked them with fresh snow from the side of the road. A fully packed canister of snow barely yielded a quarter canister of water, we had to repeat this process quite often in order to keep ourselves alive.

We resumed the march that seemed endless to us. How could they possibly want to use us to dig trenches and make fortifications for them when they were starving us to death, I asked my father. He responded by saying, "Do you really expect logic and reasonable thinking from bestial criminals like the Nazis? Don't expect anything from them, and you won't be disappointed." I asked my father again about hiding in the hay tonight. He said that we first had to get an idea of where we were in relation to where my mother was located; otherwise we would be wandering around in a strange place and be handed over to the Nazis. They would just execute us on the spot. I felt, however, that at some point we would have to take a chance and escape. Otherwise, we would die of starvation or dysentery.

Night was approaching, time for me to grab a blanket from one of the corpses before we turned off onto a country road leading to an abandoned village. As we turned off the main highway, a pair of Russian planes started strafing the German convoys. People were running in all directions, as clouds of smoke and flames were billowing skyward from the German convoy.

The Nazis kept us marching towards the village and would whip anyone who turned around to see the carnage on the main highway. By now we were familiar with the routine of the stampede, we locked arms bracing for it. It helped stem the pressure from behind us so that fewer prisoners were trampled to death. We fell into a deep sleep as soon as we hit the hay. It was a long, exhausting day of walking in snow and sleet. We did not dare take our treasured leather shoes off for fear that someone would steal them while we were asleep. We were fortunate not to be afflicted by the sickness and diseases that affected most of the prisoners. My father told me to count my blessings, considering what was taking place all around us.

Wednesday, January 24, 1945

At the crack of dawn the sirens went off while the SS guards were standing at the barn door rushing us to line up for the march. It took a while before all the prisoners were assembled. Even the mean-spirited SS guards realized by now that these prisoners were a bunch of emaciated men in their final stages of life.

The column of haggard prisoners was moving to the main highway for another day of the same painfully tortuous march. The column was visibly shorter as a result of all these people dying of starvation and dysentery. The column was halted before entering the main highway to allow priority passage for several military convoys. This gave us a chance to replenish our canisters with freshly packed snow. As we moved onto the highway, I tossed my blanket, enabling me to move more freely.

This was the fourth day of this agonizing march, with no end in sight. The scene on the road was the same as the day before. We were now experiencing pangs of hunger and feeling the effects of starvation. It was getting more difficult to walk. I would get into a momentary daze and kept walking like a zombie. It was like my mind was wandering off somewhere and suddenly came back to reality. I was afraid that I was becoming afflicted with something, but I didn't know what it was. I did not want to tell my father about it and get him worried. I tried hard to gather all my faculties and act normal so that my father would not notice that something was happening to me. I did not understand the symptoms, nor did I know how to react to them or if I had the wherewithal to react to them.

We were walking by a farm, and suddenly I saw this German farmer dump a bucket of small potatoes at the prisoners. The prisoners fell upon them like a bunch of vultures. I managed to catch a small potato that was still warm. I remember hesitating if I should share this potato with my father. To this day I have mixed feelings about that occurrence. I feel guilty for having hesitated whether I should share it with my father. Yet I feel proud that I overcame my animal instincts and shared it with my father. It is extremely difficult for people under normal circumstances to comprehend how depravity and hunger can bring out the animal instinct in people and what it takes to overcome it. Those were trying circumstances that differentiated the beast from the man. My father, for example, didn't even join the prey.

As we marched past the village, we came across an intersection with clear road markings. This gave us an idea of where we were and of the direction in which we were going. It so happened that the road sign with an arrow pointing in the same direction we were going read, "Neisse-Neustadt 36 km." I suddenly perked up and turned to my father saying, "Look at this sign. We are only 36 kilometers (22.5 miles) away from my mother. We must do something about it and get away from this disastrous march." He said that this was quite some distance away. We could be caught and executed many times over if we were not careful. We also had to make sure not to jeopardize mother's safety. We must be cautious and plan it carefully.

This certainly was enough to dampen my excitement. Well, at least for a while. I wasn't quite ready to take no for an answer. I persisted in pursuing it later on when he would be more receptive to the idea. I just had to bite my time. The daylight was dimming; time to fetch another blanket from a corpse before we veered off the highway into another abandoned village. We turned off the highway onto a country road. I could see lights in the distance. This must be the village we were going to. My mind was racing a mile a minute and I forgot to check the road sign for the direction to Neisse. I was trying to find a way to convince my father to make the escape.

We were near the barn now and the stampede was in full force, which we managed to stem by locking our arms and slowing it down. Luckily the force had gotten weaker, because the men got weaker and didn't have the strength to push. We flopped down on the hay and rested for a moment to catch our breath. I started to tell my father that at some point we must take a chance. Nobody was going to do it for us; time was running out. Our strength was gone; we had to create our opportunity now. We should bury ourselves in the hay before the SS guards came around with their dogs and sirens.

My father said, "Look, we are getting closer to Neisse all the time. Why don't we wait one more day and then see where we are?" I said, "OK, Dad, we will wait one more day, but than we must go for it! This procrastination does not get us any-where." I fell into a deep, peaceful sleep, hoping that finally we had made a decision to take some action.

Thursday, January 25, 1945

The sirens shrieked, the SS guard with the dog at his side holding a whip in the other hand was standing by the open doors of the barn, yelling, "Macht schnell, macht schnell!" (Hurry up, hurry up!). The cold morning air with a strong chilling wind made us shiver as soon as we got outside for the line up. There was a dusting of snow from the night before, but not enough to accumulate at the bottom of the wooden soles that most prisoners wore. This time the blanket surely came in handy to wrap around me. People were stumping their feet to keep from freezing.

We packed our canisters once again with snow and were glad to see the column moving. This time we walked without a stop onto the main highway. I was unable to see the markings on the road sign because it was wind blown with snow. My father said he thought we were walking in the direction of Neisse, but he couldn't be 100% sure. Even in this freezing weather the road was filled with German woman and children running away from the Russians. There were very few men among the German civilians, because most of the men had been mobilized into the army.

Overhead, Russian planes were flying sorties and attacking the military convoy. They must have noticed us and recog-nized the concentration camp uniforms. They did not dive to attack any trucks in the vicinity of our column. The death rate among the prisoners must have reached into the hundreds per day. It was just so sad to see the end of the war so near and yet so far for us.

The march was painstakingly arduous. It was increasingly impossible to keep up with the pace of the march in the emaciated state we were in. The column started thinning out with people dying en mass on the side of the road. Their feet couldn't hold them up any longer. This was the fifth day of a continuous march without food or water. Most prisoners were emaciated to start with; there was no reserve weight or fat to shed. There is a limit to what the human body can endure. We, by far, exceeded that limit.

It was obvious that we had reached the breaking point. It was horrible to witness human suffering on that scale. I was starting to get symptoms of diarrhea and that scared me. I knew that this was akin to a death sentence. I did not want to tell my father about it, nor did I want him to go through the pain of seeing me collapse in front of him. It was a hopeless situation when even I was looking for a miracle to happen.

We just kept walking along in the same melancholy rhythm, waiting for the day to end and to rest in a barn. When we approached another intersection with a road sign clearly marked, we saw that Neisse was now only 24 km (15 miles) from here. I turned to my father and said to him, "That is it! We must hide in the hay tonight. We cannot wait any longer." At night, the Nazis lead us into a side road to an abandoned village. The usual stampede ensued, and we made it to the hay in one piece, thank goodness. My father and I decided to hide in the hay at the crack of dawn.

10 MY ESCAPE

Friday, January 26, 1945

At 5:00 a.m., while it was still pitch dark, the sirens were ablaze and two Nazi guards with a Kapo burst the barn gates wide open, rushing the prisoners to line up. Their flash lights were blinding us, and there was no way we could hide in the hay now! We were forced to leave the barn with the rest of the prisoners for the line-up.

The prisoners just couldn't muster enough strength to join the column with the speed the Nazis expected. They were beaten by the Nazi guards and attacked by their dogs to expedite the process. We were standing in the freezing weather, waiting for all the prisoners to join the column.

Daylight appeared on the horizon, helping us find our orientation into which direction we were going. As the column started to march towards the main highway, a squadron of Russian planes appeared, silhouetted against the bright eastern sky. Soon afterwards, we could feel the shaking and could hear loud explosions in the distance. The Nazis didn't even stop us from marching towards the highway. We continued walking.

As we reached the intersection, we were suddenly stopped. I could clearly see the road sign. It pointed to the left and read, "Neisse 24 km." Our lead column was turned to the right, which was the opposite direction of Neisse. While we were standing at the intersection, my father asked ten men to stand together, so that he could conduct the Shachris (morning prayers) and say the Kaddish (the mourning prayer commemorating the anniversary of death). It was the anniversary of my grandfather's death. In order to recite the Kaddish, there had to be a quorum (a Minyan) of ten men over the age of thirteen.

While my father was getting the quorum together and praying, I found out why the Nazis had stopped us right at the intersection: German soldiers were leading a long column of French POWs on the main highway, walking in the direction of Neisse.

What was taking place at the intersection at this particular moment is almost indescribable. I will try my best to describe the scene and the sequence of events.

The column of concentration camp prisoners was turning right, walking in the opposite direction of Neisse. When the column was stopped, we were in the middle of the intersection. My father got together a quorum of ten men so that he could recite the memorial prayer in honor of my grandfather. On the curb to our left stood a group of 11-to-13-year-old Hitler-Jugend (Hitler Youth) boys, watching the spectacle of emaciated prisoners in their striped uniforms.

On the main road, German soldiers were leading a column of French POWs. At this moment, the SS guard watching us turned around with his back to us, looking for something in his horse-led sled. I could see the end of the column of the French POWs passing us. This was my chance! I quickly tore off my striped uniform, dropping it on the road. Now I was dressed in the French woolen sweater and cap. I hurriedly poked my father on the elbow while he was reciting the Kaddish, and said to him in Yiddish: "Tate, ich gei." (Dad, I'm going).

I walked right past the Hitler-Jugend (Hitler Youth) cursing in German, "Die verfluchten Juden!" (Those damned Jews!) and walked straight toward the column of the French POWs. In my French sweater and woolen cap, I could have passed as a French prisoner. I had escaped!

The problem now was that I found myself between the hammer and the anvil. I was too young to be a French POW. Suddenly, I had terrible cramps, an attack of diarrhea! Luckily, I was able to run behind the snow bank on the side of the highway, when my guts literally gushed out of me and I must have passed out. To this day, I have no recollection of how long I was laying in the snow or what made me come to and wake up. I attribute it all to my grandfather's spirit working on my behalf. He had prayed for me at my bedside when I was a boy and had my ruptured appendix removed. There just might be some supernatural connection. Who knows? Maybe it is only human nature to be cleansed after such a gut wrenching experience. It felt like I was revived from the dead.

I was still in a daze from the transformation that just occurred. From behind the snow bank I had a good view of what was taking place on the road while the people on the road could not see me. All I was able to see was the heavy civilian traffic and German military convoys. Then I noticed two Ukrainian soldiers that had served in General Vlasov's army. (General Vlasov defected with his entire army from the Red Army, to serve the Germans). They were now running away from the advancing Russian forces, towards the Americans.

I approached them and begged them to give me a piece of bread. They pulled out a piece of bread from their backpack and handed it to me. I thanked them for the bread. When I attempted to eat it, I realized that it was frozen like a rock. My teeth were not strong enough to bite into it. I must have been in much worse condition than I thought.

Now I was confronted with a situation my father and I had discussed frequently in the camp: careful planning as an essential part of a successful escape. However, it was not only the escape itself but the aftermath that must be laid out in detail and well planned. As I was thinking about these words, I said to myself, "My escape would have never happened if I had taken time to plan." There are situations in life when you have to act instinctively and go by your gut feelings or else you die.

This was the kind of conversation I had with myself as I was wondering how to find my mother. The first thing I decided to do was to try to get lost in the crowd and continue walking in the direction of Neisse. There were thousands of people on the road. They were traveling by car, riding on a horse sled, and walking on foot. In addition, there were military convoys traveling in both directions. There was no problem getting lost in this setting as long as no one talked to me. I worried that, by some chance, someone might discover who I was.

Frequently, the Russian planes would dive down right over the German convoys and shoot at the soldiers in them. Whenever this happened, the civilians would run into the fields on the side of the road until the raid was over. I, too, took cover with the civilians on the side of the road. Now that I did not have my tin canister, I had to eat snow to quench my thirst while on the side of the road.

My hunger pains were getting the best of me, especially when I watched the German peasants feasting on Bratwurst und Kartoffelsalat (smoked sausage and potato salad). As I was walking, I smelled a strong aroma of food being cooked getting closer and closer. I turned around and saw a military field kitchen on a horse-driven sled. In front, there was a bench on which a German guard and a French POW were sitting. In the rear of the sled there was a large kettle with burning coal underneath, heating the food, with a stoop in the back of it.

I quickly stepped onto the rear stoop reaching over the kettle and tapped the French chef on the shoulder telling him in my broken French: "I'm a Jew. I just escaped from the march. Could you please give me a piece of bread?" The chef gave me a large bowl of hot soup and a large slice of bread with lots of melted cheese on top. I thanked him several times and went to the side of the road to feast on this bounty. I am at a total loss to describe the feelings of gratitude and satisfaction I had when eating that soup. To say that it was sublimely heavenly would not adequately do it justice. You would have to be in similar circumstances to understand the level of elation a meal like this could provide to a starving human being.

The fact that my stomach blew up like a balloon because it was my first hot food in six days didn't matter at all. What mattered was being able to have a heavenly experience with

116

food. The thing that saddened me the most was the fact that I could not share that meal with my father.

The transformation in my mood and energy that this meal produced was phenomenal. I grabbed a hold of a horse-driven sled with German peasants and was gliding along the highway for a few miles until they went off the road. The Russian planes were harassing the German convoys non-stop.

The civilians, and I among them, kept running back and forth into the fields for cover. A German woman started talking to me immediately after the raid saying, "The Jews are responsible for the war! They are financing all the armament industries of Russia and America." She went on and on. It was obvious that she repeated the Nazi propaganda word for word. What was worse, she believed it and was convinced that it was true. I of course could not say anything. I spoke German with an obvious accent and did not want to raise any suspicions. I just listened and kept walking along until another air raid forced us off the road again and I lost her.

When I returned to the road, another woman started a conversation with me complaining and blaming the Jews. She told me that her family had lived in this area for many generations. I asked her for directions to Neisse and the area in general. She told me that Neisse was the name of a river that divides the town, and that the German army was building fortifications to stop the Russian advance. She gave me precise directions to Neisse-Neustadt. I grabbed a hold of the rear of the next horse-driven sled going in the direction of Neisse. They veered off to a side road on the outskirts of the town; I had to walk by myself into the town. The town was deserted; I saw very few people.

As I came closer to the town, I realized that this highway lead straight to a bridge that crossed the river. Based on the instructions the woman had given me, I would have to cross that bridge in order to reach my mother's address. The problem was that the German military were building fortifications around the river, and there was a sentry stationed on both sides of the river. I had no choice now, I had to face the sentry and cross the bridge.

In my mind, I fabricated all sorts of questions the guard at the sentry may ask me, none of which made any sense. In any case, I decided to cross that bridge when I got to it. I observed for a while how they checked other people and vehicles as I was walking towards the bridge. I had to give the impression of being a part of this area. I went straight towards the guard at the sentry booth. He stopped me and said, "Ausweis, bitte." (Identification, please.) I replied to him in German with a heavy French accent, "I was working for a German farmer on the outskirts of Gleiwitz. We were on a horse-drawn sled escaping the war zone when during a Russian air raid we run into the fields for cover. We lost each other in the confusion. I could not find my boss. He has all my papers. Now I am looking for work. Could you please direct me to an employment office in Neisse where they would assign me to a local farmer?"

The guard kept repeating that I must have my ID card with me, and I pretended that I had trouble understanding him, that all I wanted was to go to the employment office and be assigned to a local farmer. Finally, he got tired of me and motioned with his arm across the bridge telling me to go ahead. This I understood immediately and crossed the bridge. Wow! What a relief that was! I don't remember how I had the nerve to carry on like this with the guard, but I did know that unlike the SS, the Wehrmacht (regular army) were fairly easy-going. I had to play my cards as best I could.

This was just another instance where one could not plan in advance. Now that I was in the town where my mother was, I had to find Klosterstraße 12 (number 12 Convent Street), which is where my mother was working as an Aryan women in the geriatric center of a Catholic convent. I had never been at a Catholic convent before, nor did I know what it looked like and what to expect. In deciding whom to ask for directions, I wanted to make sure not to raise any suspicions that might endanger my mother's safety.

11 FINDING MY MOTHER

I decided to ask a young teenager for directions, reasoning that he wouldn't have the savvy to be suspicious. As soon as the thought crossed my mind, a young boy came out into the street. I approached him and asked him where Klosterstraße 12 was. He told me, pointing to the church, that as soon as I passed the church I was to turn right onto Klosterstraße. I followed his directions, and as I passed the church, I saw the street sign: Klosterstraße.

As I turned right, I saw an ornate wrought iron fence with a decorative gate and the number 12. My heart started beating in anticipation like a drum. I went through the wrought iron gate to the carved grand entrance of the building. As I walked up the two granite steps leading to the door, I was debating whether I should ring the bell or just knock on the door. I decided to open the door quietly and take a peek to see what was going on inside. My heart was beating double time.

I grabbed the door handle and opened the door just enough to see a very large foyer. The floor boards were polished wide planks of wood, across from the door was a stairway with a beautiful wide wooden banister, on the left side of the door I saw a huge wooden sculptured cross of Christ, on the right side of the door was a wall and a large opening where the stairwell started. There was an eerie stillness in the place; I did not quite know what to make of it. I made sure that my shoes were clean and dry before walking into the foyer.

I walked in and stood on the left side of the door right underneath the cross waiting for someone to come. While I was standing there, I was thinking of the irony of the situation.

Here I was, a persecuted Jew, seeking shelter under the very symbol that was responsible for centuries of Jewish persecution. At last I saw a lady dressed in a white uniform walking down the stairs straight into that other room. I don't know if she even noticed me standing underneath the cross. If she did she probably disregarded me. I waited in that eerie stillness a while longer, and the same lady came out of that room with a teakettle in her hand and a tray with cookies.

I ran out of patience. Before she started walking up the stairs, I said to her in German, "Excuse me, please." She turned back and came towards me. I asked her in German, "Do you know a women by the name of Barbara Siegmund?" She came even closer to me and replied, "Yes, I am Barbara Siegmund. Who are you?" I responded in Yiddish, saying, "Mama, don't you recognize me?" I reached for the cookies on the tray and tried to take the teakettle from her hand. She stopped me and told me to go outside and wait for her; she would take care of everything.

While waiting for my mother outside, I was wondering why neither one of us had recognized the other. The answer was quite simple: in spite of the miserable conditions in the concentration camp, I had grown and was now taller than my mother. The white nurses uniform my mother wore might have had something to do with it as well.

When she came out, she started walking and told me that this was a geriatric institution. She was bringing tea and cookies to serve to a German couple that came to pick up their father and take him west. She thought that I was their chauffeur. My mother took me to another convent in the same town, where my aunt Sarah was working as an Aryan. That convent was primarily an agricultural one with a farm, cow stables and a barn. They also had summer and winter residences. In the winter, the summer residence was vacant. This was where my aunt Sarah decided to hide me until the war ended.

Three days after my arrival, two more prisoners that had escaped from the Death March were brought over by my mother for my aunt to hide. These were the men my father had used as middleman to correspond with my mother. We hoped and expected that my father would also escape and join us. It was with great regret and sorrow that we learned from concentration camp survivors later that my father had died en route to the concentration camp of Gross-Rosen.

Guilt plays an interesting role in the Judeo Christian tradition in which we were brought up. You are damned if you do and damned if you don't. I cannot count the number of times I have been flagellating myself with feelings of guilt that I saved myself and abandoned my father to perish on the Death March. It was, and continues to be, a heavy burden for me to carry. The question always arises: you were able to do it when you grabbed your cousin Janek and escaped, why didn't you grab your father with you? It is easy for a person unaffected by the interplay of events of the moment to make observations or even judgments about my guilt or innocence on the way I acted. I myself have been tortured by feelings of guilt time and time again even though I'm thoroughly convinced that under the circumstances of the moment I could not have acted differently. Just examining the risk of getting shot or discovered was enough to prevent one from committing an act of insanity like an escape.

That is exactly what it was, an act of insanity that miraculously worked out well. It is OK to go crazy and play Russian roulette with your own life, but it is irresponsible to do it with another person's life. This is my rationalization, and it doesn't always work. Aunt Sarah took upon her the enormous risks of taking care of three refugees under very difficult circumstances.

She worked as a farm hand in this convent and was taking care of her niece Ruzia, uncle Moses's older daughter. She had to be extremely careful that other farm hands did not discover her activities that were dangerous and difficult. Because we were hiding in a summer residence, there was no running water in the winter. We had to deposit all our excrements in a metal bucket that she would empty every morning and mix in with the cow manure. Fortunately, she started her work shift at 4:00 a.m., when no one was around to see her switching buckets.

She would bring us fresh milk when she milked the cows and bring hot potatoes that she had boiled for the pigs, along with some hard-boiled eggs made from eggs she had taken from the hens. We hoped that it would take a few days to a week for the Russians to cross the Oder and Neisse rivers and liberate us.

Unfortunately the Russians halted their offensive until the beginning of March. This made it extremely difficult and dangerous for aunt Sarah. She did a miraculous job of keeping us alive and safe for six weeks until the beginning of March. During the weeks in which we were sheltered by aunt Sarah in the summer residence of the convent, we had no opportunity to take a bath. The lice and crabs nested on our emaciated bodies, keeping us busy for days on end hunting for them.

The Russians started an intensive artillery attack on the entire region. Russian planes attacked German anti-aircraft batteries and any military targets they could find. During the bombing of an anti-aircraft battery the Germans operated behind the convent, all the windows in the summer residence were shattered. Aunt Sarah came to us and told us to leave the summer residence and go into the barn. She asked us not to leave together; only one person at a time. When we met there we should find a spot in the upper section of the barn. She would be in touch with us and take care of everything. As it happened, the barn was a lot closer to the cow stables, which made it easier for aunt Sarah to take care of us. We met in the barn and found a spot under the rafters of the tiled roof. We wanted aunt Sarah to be more relaxed about everything. We told her not to worry; in case we were caught, we would tell our captors that we had escaped from the march and broke into this barn.

Things were going quite well for a few days, until the Russian planes that attacked the anti-aircraft batteries near the convent were strafing the tiles off the roof above us. We were extremely lucky not to be injured. It would have been a tragedy for us to escape the Death March and then get killed in this barn by Russian bullets. We had to run down to the lower barn, where we were discovered by one of aunt Sarah's coworkers who happened to speak Polish. We gave him the prepared story that we had escaped and broken into the barn.

He called aunt Sarah into the barn to consult her and introduce her to us. She acted surprised to see these three Jewish men. She suggested that we seek shelter in one of the abandoned German homes and offered to take us to one. We accepted her offer and thanked them both for being so kind to us. When we were a safe distance away, she told us that she was taking us to an abandoned house in the vicinity of the convent where my mother worked. She was thankful that her coworker didn't question our story or suspect her involvement with us. She pointed to an abandoned house that was around the corner from Klosterstraße, where my mother worked. We thanked her for all her hard work and for the risks she was taking to save our lives.

I climbed through an unlocked window on the side of the house and then unlocked the main entrance for my friends to enter. The house was immaculate. The first thing we looked for was food and water. We found everything in good order; we even managed to get the water heater going after several attempts. We looked at each other and started joking, "You mean to tell me that you are going to put on the same clothing with the lice on your body?" We had to find some Lysol to disinfect ourselves, and then find a change of clothing. What we couldn't find in this house, we found in other houses in the neighborhood. We had to keep a low profile in order not to get caught. The place was like a ghost town, totally abandoned, with the exception of the seniors in the convent where my mother worked.

My mother came to check on us. My aunt had told her where we were. I told my mother not to worry about us; we would take care of ourselves. She told us that the priest was conducting a prayer service and mass in the basement of the convent, we could come over there and pretend to be Catholic and participate in the service. I told her that as soon as we get settled and cleaned up, we would explore all possibilities. I told her not to go outside to visit us with all this artillery fire and strafing going on.

I promised that I would come as a good Catholic to pray at her convent. She had a big smile on her face and left. We had all the Lysol and fresh clothing we needed. Getting rid of the old clothing was simple enough, but getting rid of the lice on our bodies was a lot more difficult and complicated. I remember that lice were one of the 10 plagues visited upon the Egyptians. I never thought of lice as a big deal until I was afflicted by them.

We had to shave off every bit of hair we had on any part of our body. Then we treated everything with Lysol, but it still wasn't enough to eliminate the lice and crabs. They were imbedded in our skin. It took quite a while, many hot baths, bottles of Lysol and burning skin to finally get rid of them. In selecting clothing to wear, we had to be careful not to look like Germans. We picked stuff that made us look like the people of Poland and that was fine with us, because we spoke Polish. We never ventured outside together, we decided where to go and then we walked there singly so as not to raise suspicion, and met at the place.

Gunfire from diving planes and artillery fire explosions were intensifying by the day. We had to be careful not to be caught in a barrage of fire. We had to go to different homes to replenish our food supplies. Fortunately, it was cold outside and the food didn't spoil. It was quite boring to hang around all day. I decided to go to the convent and volunteer to help out with certain chores. No one had any inkling that my mother and I were related. I was given cooked meals while working. I even decided to join the service while the priest was conducting Mass. It was an interesting scene.

In the basement of the convent, a collection of elderly people, some seated in chairs, others in wheel chairs with nurses at their side, were listening to the priest. All this to the accompanying sounds of exploding artillery shells all around us. The priest was saying something in Latin and then came around inserting a small wafer into the mouths of the worshippers. For a minute, I was wondering if it was Kosher for me to accept this wafer. Then I thought to myself, you better accept it if you don't want to raise any suspicion. Fortunately for me, at the time, I did not know the symbolic significance of the wafer. Had I known it, I would have avoided taking it. I guess sometimes "ignorance is bliss." I just wondered whether I had to be so blissful. One more thought came to my mind: what would be my father's reaction, seeing his son participating in a Catholic Mass. Besides, one is always allowed to cross certain taboos for the sake of survival. When I left the convent to return to the abandoned home where we were staying, I encountered a barrage of artillery fire with shells falling and exploding all around me. The entire place was blanketed with exploding artillery shells and the whizzing sound of diving Russian planes bombing German ground targets wherever they could find them. It looked and sounded like all hell broke loose. For a minute, I considered returning to the convent where I would be safer. I decided to make a run for it, and fortunately, I was not hit by the fire or by any flying debris.

At the house, the other men were rejoicing at the intensive artillery and air attacks. They opened a bottle of Schnapps to celebrate the upcoming liberation. The schnapps helped us get a good night's sleep, only to wake up to loud, hard knocking on the door. When we opened the door, we were confronted by several Russian soldiers questioning us and wondering who we were. We spoke Polish and showed them the tattooed concentration camp numbers on our forearm. Their attitude changed completely. They told us that we could start our journey home whenever we chose to. All of us jumped for joy, hugging the Russian soldiers and thanking them.

I immediately went over to meet my mother at the convent. When we met, we were finally able to hug each other without any fears of divulging our relationship. It was natural and genuine! I had longed for this hug for over two-and-a-half years. All of a sudden, I got mushy and my eyes started tearing like a baby and my emotions got the best of me. It felt good to finally let go and express the pain and accept my mother's love.

We were both hopeful that my father and my older brother Moses David would survive the war and join us in Jaworzno. We had no idea whether or not there would be any means of transportation. We just decided to take the most essential items and get on the road going east towards Poland. We figured that in the worst-case scenario, we would stay at night in abandoned German homes until we reached Poland. My mother came down with two huge stuffed bags to start the journey. I looked at the bags and turned to my mother, saying, "These bags will just weigh us down; we will not be able to walk with them." We did not need any of this; all we needed was our freedom to go to Jaworzno as soon as possible. My mother relented, and we started our journey walking towards the main highway.

The main highway was clogged with Russian military vehicles ranging from horse-drawn sleds to heavy tanks. While most of the military traffic was going west, there were some military vehicles that traveled east. There were many German civilians that were caught up by the Russian advance and had to return east to their homes.

We were hopeful that we would be able to hitch a ride on one of the military vehicles going east towards Poland. We were walking for several hours, trying to flag down one of the military vehicles. Finally, one of the vehicles with two soldiers in the front cabin stopped for us. My mother was asked to go in the front cabin while they asked me to climb up onto the truck. We were on our way. I was happy that we had a ride and started visualizing our arrival in Jaworzno. The thoughts of my father and brother coming home to unite the family were running through my mind. I was also wondering how aunt Sarah and Ruzia were doing. I even branched out thinking about many other members of our extended family, wondering how many of them would have managed to survive.

Our extended family in Jaworzno had consisted of about 108 people. It would be nice to reconnect and unite the family. After a while, I decided to peek into the cabin window to see how my mother was doing. I saw that there was some sort of commotion going on. There was some wrangling between the driver of the truck and my mother who was on the right side of the cabin. I immediately knocked on the drivers window asking him to stop the truck. As the truck was coming to a halt, I climbed to the other side and opened the door so that my mother could get out, but the driver held on to my mother's hand and would not let go of her. I went over to the driver's side and tried to plead with him to let go of my mother. He swung the door open and pulled out a machine gun, aiming at me like he was going to shoot me. Fortunately there was a ditch on the side of the road that I jumped into and moved away from his angle of view; the other soldier in the cabin prevented him from shooting at me. While he was busy with me, my mother was able to get out, and the truck left.

My mother asked me to join her and get going because it was getting late in the day. Suddenly, I was unable to move my left leg; I had such sharp pain. I didn't know if the pain was caused by this shocking experience of sudden fright. I just could not walk. My mother had to go to one of the abandoned homes to find a baby carriage so that she could wheel me the rest of the way. It took quite a while before she got back with a carriage. I started to worry. She brought some towels with her so that I could wrap them around my leg and immobilize it. It was hard to slide out of the ditch on my rear. I was able to do it by lifting myself on my hands and swing backwards. Once I was out of the ditch, my mother helped me get up and into the carriage. At this time it started to get dark outside and my mother wheeled me to an abandoned home off the road where we spent the night. My mother tried all sorts of compresses on my leg, from ice to hot, to see which would make me feel more comfortable. The ice seemed to have a numbing effect on the leg, which temporarily reduced the pain. She scraped together some food and made a meal.

For the first time in two-and-a-half years my mother and I were together. She explained to me that the Russian driver had been drunk and could not be held responsible for his actions. She said it was good that the other soldier was able to control him and that we got away. These soldiers were away from their families for months, fighting a cruel war. They were drowning their sorrow in vodka, and this was the result of it. We tried to figure out how many members of our family would return and how we were going to reestablish our roots and settle in Jaworzno. I told my mother that Jaworzno and, for that matter, all of Poland, was drenched with Jewish blood, and that it would be unlikely that any of us would be happy staying in Poland. If we had to start anew, we should do it in the Promised Land. That is where our ancestors came from, and that is where we had to return. Enough of being subjected to persecution and humiliation. It was time to stand up for ourselves!

My mother had never before seen those feelings so strongly expressed by me. She did not realize how hurt and violated I felt by all this persecution and, most of all, by the submissiveness of the Jewish masses going like sheep to the slaughterhouse. I felt better after sharing my feelings with her and got them off my chest. I had a good night's sleep in spite of the pain in my leg every time I turned. We got up in the morning, had a quick breakfast and were ready to move on. I did not feel comfortable that my mother had to wheel me around like a baby, but I had no choice, and I was confident that in time my leg would heal. The distance from where we were to Jaworzno was about 120 km or 75 miles, which was a long distance to wheel a 15.5-year-old boy in a baby carriage. Gleiwitz, a large German town about 15 km east of us, would be our next stop.

My mother decided that once we reached Gleiwitz she would wheel me straight into the Russian commander's office and ask him to provide us with transportation to Jaworzno. The determination of my mother was not something to argue with. She had the endurance of a tiger and the strength of a lioness. This is what got her treading the snow-laden roads to the Blechhammer concentration camp. I was the payoff of that determination. It took most of the day for us to reach Gleiwitz. My mother decided that it was best to meet the local military commander the next morning rather than in the late evening. We went into another abandoned home to stay overnight.

The Russians had occupied the town two weeks before we arrived; everything was still very confusing. The Deutsche Mark (German Mark) was still used as currency in some places while the Polish Zloty was used in others. Fortunately, my mother had saved a substantial amount of the Deutsche Mark, so that she was able to buy food and other basic items. She wanted us to see a doctor before we went to the Russian commander. My mother's perfect German was helpful in finding a doctor. I had a severe muscular inflammation in my leg. He suggested that we heat some sand bags in the oven and use them as a compress on the leg. I was told to exercise by doing knee bends in a lying position and that in six weeks I would be able to walk again.

When we got to the Russian commander in Gleiwitz, he turned to my mother and said, "What is a beautiful woman like you doing in this godforsaken place?" My mother looked at him with a smile and said in Yiddish, "You think if I had a choice, I would be here?" He looked at her and said, "What makes you think that I understand Yiddish?" My mother replied, "With a nose like that, what else could you be?" He laughed and said, "So, what can I do for you?" in plain Yiddish. She told him that we were heading to Jaworzno. He arranged for us to get a ride to Katowice, which was about 15 miles from Jaworzno. "From there," he said, "you can take a bus to Jaworzno." He arranged for my mother to exchange Deutsche Marks for Zlotys, which was the Polish currency used in Katowice. My mother thanked him for his generous services, and we were on our way to Katowice.

When we arrived in Katowice, we found out that there was no regular bus service going to Jaworzno as yet. The only mode of transportation was either horse-drawn carriages or trucks that carried supplies between the two cities. The distance between Katowice and Jaworzno was only about 15 miles, so my mother arranged for us to be taken to Jaworzno by a freight truck later that day. She wanted first to contact members of the Jewish community in Katowice to find out what kind of assistance was available to Jewish survivors.

Katowice was a city with a sizeable Jewish community. She figured that they would be able to advise her on the laws and practices instituted by the Communist regime in Poland. The Jewish community association of Katowice prepared my mother for what was to happen once she would reach Jaworzno. They told her point blank, "You will not be able to go into your own home if it is occupied by a Polish family. You will not be able to retrieve any of your possessions that are now used by a Polish family. If you have something hidden or buried in your house, you will not be able to claim it without the permission of the present occupants. The best the Polish town hall will do for you is find you accommodations with other Jewish survivors in Jewish homes that were unoccupied or abandoned." Being forewarned is being forearmed. This advice was helpful in preparing my mother for all eventualities. Now we were able to leave Katowice to go to Jaworzno.

12 RETURN TO JAWORZNO

Not being able to walk hampered my mobility to a large extent. I was unable to carry anything, because I had to use a cane to take the weight off my injured leg. It was faster to get around when I was wheeled in a carriage. My mother wheeled me to the spot where the truck drivers pick up passengers to ride with them in their cabin. The drivers made extra money by ferrying passengers to the various destinations. It was the immediate aftermath of the war. Public transportation and bus services were not functioning yet. Everyone had to make private arrangements. We waited at that spot for over half an hour, during which time various drivers stopped by and announced their destinations to the waiting passengers.

Finally, a driver stopped and yelled, "do Jaworzno" (to Jaworzno). My mother went over to him and pointed to me while negotiating the price. I had to be helped getting into the cabin while the driver loaded the carriage into the truck, and we were on our way to Jaworzno. My mother had a very animated conversation with the driver telling him about us. She asked him many questions about what was going in Jaworzno and who was in charge of town hall. She also inquired if there were any Jews that had returned to Jaworzno and where they lived. He explained to my mother that everything was controlled and run by the local Communist party. He suggested that we be dropped off at the local town hall and my mother get all the pertinent information and directions from them. The landmark of Jaworzno, the huge chimneys of the coalmines, appeared on the horizon, and we knew we had arrived.

We asked the driver to turn into Mickiewicza Street from Jagielonska Street, just so we could take a peek at our house. As we passed the school, my heartbeat accelerated just by looking at our house on 11 Mickiewicza Street. My mother asked the driver to stop for a moment so that we could see if there was any sign of life. We decided not to get off at our house and went straight to town hall. My mother paid the driver and thanked him. She asked the driver to help me get off the truck and put me in the carriage while she went into the offices to make arrangements so that we could get accommodations. She informed the authorities that aunt Sarah and Ruzia should be coming any day and asked them to accommodate us together. They informed her that Sarah and Ruzia were already in town and that they had requested the same for us.

We were given an address that was the old Laufer residence, located behind the church. My mother wheeled the carriage across the Rynek (market place) past my grandfather's house to the Laufer's residence. Passing by my grandfather's house, we saw that the pharmacy was still there. The stationery store, which had been owned by our grandfather, had been replaced by a hardware store. The house was occupied by vagrants who were supported and supervised by social services of town hall. It was impossible for us to gain permission to enter the premises. When we reached the Laufer residence, we were greeted by aunt Sarah, Ruzia and a survivor of the Laufer family. There was enough room to accommodate us comfortably. We gave aunt Sarah the details of our adventurous trip to Jaworzno and settled in for the night.

The following morning my mother took me to our old family doctor to check out my leg. Oddly enough, he came up with the same diagnosis and the identical remedies of burlap sacks with sand. The only difference was that he asked that I keep my legs elevated.

The period of waiting and hoping for family members to return home was extremely painful. Every time someone knocked on the door, we hoped that it was one of our relatives coming to join us. It was disappointing to see the door opening and not seeing a survivor entering. Nights we were sitting and contemplating the probabilities of some of our loved ones surviving. We knew that my father had been alive on January 26, 1945. We were hoping that my brother Moses David would survive the war. It was a difficult time for the entire family. It was especially hard for me because of the guilt feelings I had for having left my father behind. These guilt feelings kept cropping up regardless of how impossible it would have been for the two us to escape together at that particular moment.

The real answer to that query is: you will never know it, unless you try it. It was not enough that I had intermittent pangs of guilt about not taking my father with me when I escaped, my mother brought up the subject during one of our conversations. She asked me, "How could you possibly escape without taking your father with you?" I was terribly shaken and hurt by this statement of my mother. I remember feeling an agonizing pain as a result of her statement. It was the first time that I burst out in tears and cried. This remark left an indelible wound in my heart. It exacerbated the guilt feelings I was dealing with all along. While I deeply loved my mother and understood her feelings, this remark would have been better left unsaid.

The need to put food on the table had to be met. Aunt Sarah was familiar with the cities of Krakow and Katowice. She decided to get involved in the black market trade between the two cities. I recovered from my leg injury and decided to join aunt Sarah in her trading activities. I accompanied her and watched her negotiate prices with currencies as well as goods. She was astute and knowledgeable about the market requirements in the two cities. I was able to help her carry goods from one place to another while I learned the tricks of the trade. The war was still being waged in full force by the Allied armies and the Russians trying to beat one another to occupy Berlin, the capital of Germany.

On May 8, 1945, the German army surrendered and the war in Europe ended. Our level of anxiety intensified, waiting to see who else might have survived the war. My mother and I were saddened and disappointed that neither my father nor my brother Mosses David had survived the war. We had a hard time adjusting to the fact that they were not alive.

Trading activity increased incrementally with the end of the war in Europe. We were now trading in currencies of the allied countries and the Russian sphere of influence countries. There was a huge demand for the US dollar and American cigarettes in Eastern Europe. The black market was thriving, and we earned a living.

I was, however, not satisfied with the way we were living. There seemed to be no meaning to our lives. We just accepted things as they were and did nothing to improve them. I felt as if my life was being wasted. Adding to my frustration were the socio-economic conditions of the Jews in post-war Poland. The entire country, including the leadership of small towns, was now under the command of Communist apparatchiks (party faithful). There was a great deal of corruption and mismanagement, and there was resentment towards returning Jewish survivors who wanted to return to their homes. Anti-Semitism was now disguised as social justice. You cannot displace people who are living in your home, just because you survived the concentration camp. You are not allowed to be compensated financially by the people who occupy your home. It was a flagrant violation directed specifically against Jews returning from years of Nazi persecution.

We waited for more than three weeks after the war ended to see if any of our relatives would return. None of them did. We had to accept our loss and cope with the inequities of life in post-war Poland. We were in contact with Jewish survivors in the other Allied-occupied parts of Europe, including West Germany. There was compassion and understanding in the treatment of Jewish survivors in the American and English spheres of influence as opposed to the discrimination practiced by the Polish post-war government.

13   THE WAY TO THE PROMISED LAND

I was not willing to accept rejection and discrimination. I did not think I was inferior as a Jew to other nationalities or religions as the anti-Semites wanted me to believe. I firmly believed that the only way this notion could be refuted was by the realization of the Zionist dream. The Jews must emigrate to the Promised Land and establish their own independent state. I was fortunate to have met in my travels to Krakow a young boy by the name of Lolek Halperin. Lolek survived the war sheltered in an orphanage in Budapest. The orphanage was run by Dr. Kotarba who received the funding for the orphanage from the Zionist organization. Lolek had traveled from Budapest to Krakow to see if any of his relatives survived the war. Unfortunately, none of them did. Lolek was disappointed and depressed that none of his close relatives had survived the war.

He explained to me in detail the activities and goals of the Zionist organization. The primary goal was to settle Jews in Palestine and create an independent national home for the Jews. He further explained to me that doing so would solve the age-old problem of persecution and discrimination against the Jews. I was enthusiastic and excited about us Jews reclaiming the historical rights in the land of our patriarchs Abraham, Isaac and Jacob. It re-ignited the spark in me that uncle Moses had implanted in me before the war to go to Palestine and escape the Nazi era of persecution.

I told Lolek that I would be in touch with him before he returned to Budapest. I made it clear to him that I intended to leave Poland and go with him to Budapest the following week. We set up a time and date to meet at the Krakow railroad station, where we would take a train together to Budapest. When I returned to Jaworzno, I told my mother that I had decided to join the Zionist movement and that I was leaving with a friend to go to Budapest next week from the Krakow rail road station. She tried very hard to dissuade me from going to Budapest. After a lengthy and painful discussion, I told her that the decision was final and irrevocable. I explained to her very straightforward that I had a sacred obligation to the memory of our lost family members and to the cause of the Jewish community at large to turn the page of Jewish history to achieve national independence. She reluctantly accepted my decision and said that she would escort me to the Krakow railroad station when I left with Lolek for Budapest.

It was not easy to just pick up and go. I had a tearful departure from my aunt Sarah and cousin Ruzia. I was comfortable with the fact that I was taking a decisive step in forming my own destiny. It was something I felt very strongly about. I would have never been at peace with myself if I did not do it. I said my final good bye as my mother and I were leaving by bus to Krakow. I was leaving with a heavy heart knowing all the things my aunt Sarah had done for me. I was fully aware that the last hurdle for me to overcome would be the final departure from my mother at the Krakow railroad station.

When we arrived at the railroad station, Lolek was waiting for me at the spot we set out to meet. I introduced Lolek to my mother. We had to board the train; we only had a few minutes left. I hugged my mother and started saying good-bye when she started crying and begging me not to leave, not to abandon her. I did not know what to do or say to my mother that would make her understand how important it was for me to go. Finally, I said to her, "Look, mom, maybe you could afford to loose a husband and three children. I don't want it to happen to me! I must do something about it!"

I immediately realized how cruel those words must have sounded to her and how bad she must feel. However, there was nothing else I could possibly say that would express my feelings more accurately than that. As the train was leaving, I saw my mother standing on the platform, crying. I deeply re-gretted having spoken to her so bluntly; I wished I could have used softer words to describe my feelings. My feelings were raw, my reality was cruel and that was all I could muster at the time.

As I was seated in the train, I remembered what my mother always used to say to me, "You are always in possession of the word you have not uttered; once you said it, it is public domain." I wish I could have said it differently, but I didn't. I felt bad to have hurt her feelings. The train was loaded to the hilt with passengers. We were lucky to have squeezed into two seats. Russian soldiers were having a field day on this train. They were robbing passengers of their valuables by jumping from one car to another over the roofs of the cars. It was total anarchy; no one could do anything about it. They were primarily interested in wristwatches and gold rings. The train made a long stop in Vienna, Austria. We did not go out into the station because we would never have gotten our seats back if we did. We were feasting on the sandwiches and cook-ies my mother had prepared for us, together with tea and lemon. The trip from Vienna to Budapest took several hours.

The scenery of the Danube River and the mountains was breathtakingly beautiful. It looked like the Russian scavengers had changed crews, but the tactics were the same. When they approached us, we told them that we already donated our watches on the first leg of the trip. During the trip Lolek briefed me on the educational program in the orphanage. It was a rich curriculum ranging from learning the Hebrew lan-guage, Jewish history, math and science as well as folk dances. Having missed two-and-a-half years of schooling, this cer-tainly would be a welcoming new experience for me. I was wondering if my lack of schooling would pose any problems in my ability to adapt to the higher level of education.

The train pulled into the Budapest railroad station and we got off to catch a bus to the orphanage. Lolek had been in Buda-pest for quite a while; he knew the city and spoke Hungarian. Lolek told me that the city was divided by the Danube River into two separate parts, Buda and Pest, connected by beautiful bridges. It really was a beautiful city. When we arrived at the orphanage, we discovered that all the children were out on a summer camp holiday in the mountains. The caretaker told Lolek that Dr. Kotarba left railway tickets for us with instructions to join the group in the mountains. We stayed overnight at the orphanage and caught a train to the mountains in the morning. The caretaker fed us well and prepared sandwiches for the trip. The trains in Hungary were clean and on schedule. It was a great trip through beautiful mountains and lakes all the way to our destination, "Silwashvarot" (to the best of my recollection). We had to take a horse-drawn wagon from the railroad station to the camp site to join the group.

The camp site was nothing like anything I had seen before. There was a large rectangular lawn with tents on either side. The youngsters were playing volleyball and soccer on the lawn. On one end of the lawn was a large tent with tables and benches, used as a dining room. I was watching the children in awe the way they were playing, free from any worries and concerns.

Lolek introduced me to Dr. Kotarba and some of the teachers. They tried to make me feel comfortable and at ease. I was completely startled by the entire scene. I had never seen or experienced that kind of playful freedom before. As I kept watching them play, I realized that these youngsters probably never had to go through the ordeals that I was subjected to for the past two-and-a-half years. Lolek and I were assigned to the same tent and got ready to join the group. It was dinnertime, and everyone assembled in the large tent where dinner was served. The majority of the children were descendants of Polish Jews who had lost their parents in the Holocaust. There were some Hungarian children as well. The language spoken among the children was predominantly Polish. Some of the Polish youngsters had been in Hungary long enough to be able to communicate in Hungarian with the local children.

After dinner all the youngsters gathered around a bond fire and sang Hebrew songs, Yiddish songs, Russian songs and even some Polish songs. They were dancing the Hora, Polka and a variety of Jewish and other folk dances. The entire atmosphere was jovial and festive. I was excited by this new experience. I hoped that I would be able to adjust to this new environment without any problems. The youngsters were eager to teach me the songs and dances, which helped me acclimate to the new environment. The ten days at the summer camp passed quickly. All of us returned by train to Dr. Kotarba's orphanage in Budapest.

The educational curriculum and the disciplined teaching environment of this orphanage were both rich and strict. It was rich because of the variety of subjects covered in meticulous detail. The great feeling about the discipline was that it came from the self-esteem of the students who generated an aura of learning and self-respect. There was a creative energy in the orphanage that manifested itself in all activities, studies, play, sports and entertainment. That certainly posed an enormous challenge for me. Not having had any formal schooling for the past two-and-a-half years forced me to attend classes with youngsters who were about two-and-a-half to three years younger than I. That didn't do much for my self-esteem.

There was this vast discrepancy between my life experiences and my lack of formal education. I had to buckle down and study hard to try to catch up with my age-level requirements. I was thankful to have received tutorials and reading materials to help me bridge the gap. It was not easy, despite my tireless efforts, to catch up. I ran into difficulties of being able to patiently accept the process. It was embarrassing for me, a 16-year old, to be in a classroom with 13-year olds. I was quite upset with myself a lot of the time and frustrated at the amount of time it took for me to advance to my age level. Feeling awkward and out of place was not my cup of tea. I made a valiant effort to make up for lost time. As the old saying goes, "What brains can't accomplish, time always will." All I needed was patience. Go and tell this to a 16-year old impetuous Meshugener (crazy) boy like me.

We all knew that the standard of living and civil liberties for Jewish survivors of Nazi persecutions were far superior in the Western occupied zone of Europe than in the Russian occupied zone consisting of East Germany, Poland, Hungary, Czechoslovakia and the Balkan countries. The Western occupied zone consisted of West Germany, France, Belgium, The Netherlands, etc. In the Western occupied zone, the Jewish survivors of Nazi concentration camps were organized by different political Zionist organizations for the purpose of emigrating and resettling in Palestine. These activities were largely supported by funds from various Jewish organizations in the USA. These organizations represented the entire spectrum of political orientation from Hashomer Hatzair (the young Guardian) on the left to (Beitar) on the right and many others in between. All of these organizations strongly emphasized the will of the survivors of the Holocaust to volunteer as emigrants and settlers to go to the land of Zion, the Promised Land.

The Zionist movement, with donations from Jews and Christians from the entire Western world, purchased parched arid tracts of land from Palestinians all over the Holy Land and converted them to a productive agricultural miracle. The revitalization of the age-old promise of returning to the Promised Land by the Jewish survivors of the Holocaust was the push necessary to break the blockade on Jewish immigration to Palestine as practiced by the British rule of Palestine under their old mandate.

In the Russian sphere of influence, Zionism as a social or political movement was outlawed. It was for this reason that Dr. Kotarba, with the consent of the Zionist organization Hashomer Hatzair (The Young Guardian), decided that it was in the best interest of the children to relocate to the American occupied zone in West Germany. This of course posed many logistical as well as legal problems. For one thing, it was illegal and forbidden to cross from the Russian occupied zone to the American occupied zone. The logistics of smuggling a group of 70 people across the border had to be worked out. The planning and organization of this operation were done with the coordinated help of all Zionist organizations.

Relocation. The gap between the decision to relocate and the implementation of it was wider than we expected. The logistics were much more complicated than we had originally assumed. The ages of the children in the orphanage ranged from two to 17 years of age. Among the adult staff of the orphanage there were a few Zionist deserters from the Russian army; one of them had an amputated leg. Dr. Kotarba, with the guidance of the Zionist organization, decided to send three of the more mature children on a fact-finding mission to Bratislava in Czechoslovakia. The three chosen for this mission were Zwiczka, Lolek and myself. Our task was to ensure that there were facilities in Bratislava large enough to accommodate our group for a short duration. The plan was to leave no later than December 10 from Budapest to Bratislava on a tour bus and stay for a few nights in the facilities we choose. We would then leave Bratislava to Prague no later than December 20, 1945. We would stay in Prague until the opportunity came to cross the border to West Germany. All of this had to be done under the guise of touring, to avoid any suspicion by the authorities. Most of the preparatory work was done by the central Zionist organization.

We went on this fact-finding mission to assure everyone that things were well prepared. I was proud to be chosen for the mission. We left by train from Budapest to Bratislava, where the representative of the Zionist team met us. Zwiczka, who was born in Bratislava and was fluent in the language, was helpful in communicating our needs to the locals. On the whole, the accommodations were not nearly as nice as the children were accustomed to at the orphanage. We figured that it would be a good lesson for the group to sacrifice some creature comforts in the process of attaining a goal. Going by bus, the group avoided being robbed by Russian soldiers on the trains. After spending two hectic days in Bratislava, we concluded that the arrangements made were adequate for our purpose. We returned to Budapest by railroad, where the Russian soldiers were roaming around, pilfering from the passengers whatever they could. Our group would be traveling by bus, so they would be spared that experience.

At the orphanage we met with Dr. Kotarba and the organizing committee for the relocation. We gave them a positive assessment of the facilities we visited in Bratislava with a detailed description of everything we had seen. It was now up to Dr. Kotarba and the Zionist organization to make final arrangements for the trip. Within three days of the meeting, we were notified that the trip would take place the following Sunday morning at 6:00 a.m. The reason for this was to make it look like a field trip going into the countryside. Everyone was instructed to take with them bare essentials only and to be ready by 6:00 a.m. sharp to leave. The excitement in the orphanage reached its peak on Saturday evening. We celebrated our departure by singing Hebrew and Yiddish songs and dancing all sorts of folk dances. We were happy that we were now getting one step closer to the Promised Land. On Sunday morning, there was no need for a rise-and-shine call. Everyone was ready to board the two buses that were waiting outside. Before the doors opened, we all stood at attention, singing the "Hatikvah," the Hebrew national anthem. We were all joyful at this emotional moment that we were taking the first step towards reaching our goal.

As the doors swung open, the kitchen staff handed out sandwiches to each of us before we climbed onto the buses. The trip was very jovial. All of us were singing and having a great time. One of the songs we were singing was, "Am Israel Chai Chai vekayam" (The Jewish people are Alive, Alive and Persevering). I was thinking a great deal about the significance of that song in its present term and in its historical context.

Here I was, among a group of children who survived a Holocaust where six million of their brethren were brutally exterminated by the Nazis. I couldn't help but ask myself the question, "What is it that we Jews have going for us, that allows us to persevere after two thousand years of exile in the Diaspora and persecutions?" The answer to that was quite interesting as I delved into it more deeply. During the Exodus from Egyptian bondage under the leadership of Moses, the Jews were given and accepted the Ten Commandments, which was the first moral code of ethical conduct known to early civilization. This was later expanded into the Torah (Pentateuch), which was enriched by the Prophets' written works, the Talmud, Mishna and many scholarly commentaries, which were added during the years of exile in the Christian and Moslem civilizations. The Jews, because of the cohesive power of their religious, moral and ethical convictions, were able to withstand centuries of persecution in the Christian as well as the Moslem societies.

There were periods during which Jews played an important role in the cultural and commercial development of both of these civilizations. The Jews of the biblical time were known as "Am Kseh Oref" (a stubborn people). The question remains: Were they able to survive for two thousand years because they were constantly harassed and persecuted? Or did they survive because of the high standards of their ethical and moral traditions? The answer clearly is that both elements played an important role in the cohesion of the Jewish people throughout the world. It was the tradition celebrated every year during the Passover Seder commemorating the Exodus from Egyptian slavery during which the Jews recite, Leshana Habaa Bjerushalayim (Next year we hope to celebrate in Jerusalem), that kept the yearning and desire to Zion alive for over two thousand years. It is this wish that we were fulfilling by our commitment to the cause of Zionism.

While all these historical facts of Jewish history were going through my mind, the bus was making its way into Bratislava, where the Zionist representatives welcomed us. Right after we got settled in Bratislava, we were informed by the Zionist representatives that by Friday morning, we were scheduled to leave by bus to Prague. The few days we spent in Bratislava passed quickly. We were given lectures by young members of the Zionist Pioneers movement from a kibbutz (communal settlement). They told us all about life and work in a kibbutz. They described to us the struggles and achievements of different settlements in the fields of agriculture and irrigation methods. They also mentioned the research done in the fields of science and technology by the Weitzman Institute and the Technion (Institute of Technology) in Haifa. We were proud to be part of a movement that strives to achieve success and autonomy for the Jewish people.

On Thursday evening we all gathered around a bond fire to celebrate our last night in Bratislava. These young members taught us new folk dances and songs. We were looking forward to our trip to Prague. On Friday morning, the buses arrived on schedule. We boarded them quickly with the young emissaries that went with us to Prague. On the way we sang the new songs they taught us the night before along with some oldies. We had a great time on our way to Prague. By the time we arrived in Prague, it was already pitch dark outside. We were assigned to different rooms in what used to be a military compound during the war and were rushed into a mess hall to receive our evening meal. We met children belonging to many different Zionist organizations waiting in that military compound for an opportunity to cross the border to the Western occupied zone of Europe.

While we were at the compound, our staff maintained a normal schedule of instructions and school activities without any interruptions. All this was done with the awareness that we had to be ready at a moment's notice to travel to the border and cross over into the American zone. We visited the various historic sites of Prague and vicinity while waiting for our turn to cross the border. Christmas in Prague was very festive and joyful. We thought that this might be a good time for us to sneak across the border.

Other groups were ahead of us and made the trip before us to be smuggled across the border. I was amazed at the organizational discipline with which the Zionist organizations had this smuggling routine worked out. Everything was planned to a T and worked like clockwork. Our turn to trek across the border came on New Year's Eve. After being in Prague for two weeks, during which we visited the city and carried on with our normal routine of studies, we were called into a meeting and told we would be bussed to the vicinity of the border late on New Year's Eve. From there we would have to walk in complete silence in deep snows for about two-and-a-half miles. We were instructed on how to take care of the small children and carry them across the snow in the forest. The Zionist emissaries emphasized the importance of absolute silence while walking in the forest. They told us that the crossing should take an hour or less from start to finish.

We were very excited to line up for the bus ride, all bundled up for a midnight crossing in the forest. We arrived at night in a dimly lit village where we lined up in a row. One of the villagers led us into the forest where the shadows of the trees mingled with the moving shadows of our bodies on the snow, which created a frightening image at first. Once we got used to the shadows moving on the surface of the snow, we were not threatened by it any more. It was a beautiful star-lit night with lights flickering in the distance. The walk was going quite well until our Russian amputee discovered one of the small children in the deep snow with his crutches. He said Kitchie, Kitchie (little one, little one). We stopped to take full count, making sure that everyone was accounted for. The walk went well considering the number of persons and their young age. It took us a little more than an hour to reach a village on the American side of the border. There were two buses waiting to take us to our new location in Ansbach, West Germany.

Once the buses started moving, we all burst out singing various Hebrew songs. We were happy to have made the trek across the border without any problems. We arrived at Ansbach at the crack of dawn to a cluster of medieval stone buildings. This was a former German officers training school. We were assigned to rooms that were prepared for us in advance. We were amazed at the organizational skill of these emissaries from the kibbutz movement; everything was meticulously planned and executed. This place was spacious and immense. Once we were settled, we learned that there were about half a dozen Zionist organizations in these facilities with about 600 children of various ages. There was fierce competition among these organizations in all sorts of sports. The overriding goal of all of us was to go to the Promised Land. Toward reaching this goal, we were given intensive lessons in Hebrew, the history and accomplishments of the pioneers in Palestine and the importance of defending our national home.

Our group was fortunate to have a first-class educational curriculum that was combined with sports and recreational activities. We were kept busy from the wee hours of the morning until late at night. Aside from the normal studies of math, science, and literature, we had many lectures on topics relating to the establishment and development of a Jewish National Home in our ancestral land of Zion. There were many lectures on land reclamation, irrigation and multiple growth cycles to maximize the productivity of the land. In addition, there were special training classes in the martial arts, teaching us various techniques of self defense. All these classes were designed to prepare us to assume a creative role of productive citizenship in our new Home Land. I was happy to have caught up in all my studies with my contemporaries. This certainly made me feel a lot more comfortable and put me in a relaxed mood.

It was now essential that I renew my ties with my mother and heal some of the wounds I inflicted during our harsh departure at the Krakow railroad station. Through the offices of the United Nations Relief Agency (UNRA), I was able to locate my mother. She was living in Zeilsheim near Frankfurt am Main in West Germany. I felt that at this time it would be appropriate for me to make amends for my previous harsh behavior and renew my ties with my mother. I did a lot of back-tracking in my mind of those events in Krakow to figure out exactly what I had done wrong, or what and how I could have done it differently. I concluded that it was not so much what I said that hurt, it was the way I said it that would have made all the difference in the world. I am not less convinced of my case now than I was at that time. The difference that time can make is important. I learned a few things in the interim and matured a little. That helped.

I decided to consult with some of my teachers and counselors to help me formulate the correct approach with my mother. I gave them a detailed description of what transpired at the Krakow railway station, along with the history of our survival. I told them how remorseful I was about the harsh words I had used and the pain that I had inflicted on my mother. It was very useful for me to get the feedback from the faculty members who through a method of role reversal put me in my mother's place and asked me, "How would you feel about everything now?" Suddenly, I realized the depth of the injury and was seeking their advice on how to handle it. The counselors and teachers gave me helpful suggestions on how to conduct myself in the conversations with my mother.

I did not contact my mother in advance of my arrival. I wanted it to be a surprise. I took the railroad to Frankfurt am Main, and from there, I took a bus to Zeilsheim. I had a bit of trouble finding the place, but I finally found it, and as I was about to ring the doorbell, I waited and wondered what kind of reception I might get. I rang the doorbell. My aunt Sarah answered the door and yelled out on top of her voice, "Shmilek is here!" My mother came running to the door, embracing me with a warm hug as tears of joy were running down her cheeks. I had grown a lot since she last saw me. She was excited and happy to see me. I received a warm welcome and reception. It helped alleviate the apprehensions I had had about this meeting. I spent several days with my mother and the rest of the family in Zeilsheim. My mother and I had calm and productive discussions about our differences. I apologized to her for my harsh behavior at the Krakow railroad station, which she gracefully accepted. We reached a point of mutual understanding and respect of each other's viewpoint, and that was fine with me.

Make-up meeting with my mother and family
in Zeilsheim, Germany. Summer 1946.

I promised my mother that I would keep in touch with her and the family by mail. I assured her that I would keep the traditions of the family in tact even though I was not a religious or orthodox Jew. I told her that I would always be faithful to the Silberberg code of ethics of honesty and decency. Even though I was a secular Jew, I inherited a sense of decency and honesty from my father. I was delighted with the outcome of that visit. I was able to make amends for my previous transgressions and create a new loving relationship with my mother. The visit with my mother helped me get a load off my chest and freed some energy to be harnessed towards the difficult tasks ahead of us.

We were waiting impatiently for our turn to leave Germany for one of the Mediterranean harbors where we could board a ship to take us to The Promised Land. A trip of this nature was complicated. The British, who had a mandate to govern Palestine, had their allegiances to the Arab oil sheikdoms that objected to the Jewish resettlement efforts in Palestine. As a consequence, they used their vast naval armada to prevent Jewish immigrants from entering the shores of Palestine. All our travels henceforth, by land or by boat, had to be done clandestinely in total secrecy, in order to elude the British secret service. It wasn't until December of 1946 when we could depart to a place unknown. The arrangements were so secretive that we had no idea where we were going. We departed stealthily in the middle of the night in what looked like military trucks with covered tarps in total silence. We traveled the entire night and the following day, only stopping in dense forests for food and relief.

It wasn't until the following night that the trucks stopped at a gate that was guarded by a member of the Haganah (the Jewish Defense forces), where a Hebrew word was used as a password. We stopped at an ornate building that resembled a mansion. We were led into the building and assigned rooms. We were so tired that we didn't care where we were; we just fell asleep. Upon waking up the following morning and walking around the walled-in area, we saw that the sign on the gate read "Saint Jerome." After some more snooping around for information, we found out that we were in Marseilles,

France. We also got the word that Saint Jerome was a former insane asylum used by the Haganah as an interim transit facility to clandestinely hide the groups destined to board ships around the Mediterranean to go to Palestine.

We did not know how long we would have to wait for a chance to board a ship for Palestine. We resumed our normal course of studies and activities; we even rehearsed for a play that we were to perform. Here we had members from the Haganah give us fitness exercises and judo lessons in the art of self-defense and a whole array of marshal arts. They also taught us how to act in case the British would board our ship as we reached the shores of Palestine. They prepared us for all possible scenarios that may occur during a British interception of our boat. This was going on until the first week of February 1947. During a play rehearsal we were told to be ready for departure in two hours at 10:00 o'clock sharp. One can hardly imagine the excitement and adrenalin that was flowing through our veins. We were finally going to realize the centuries-old dream of our forefathers as they recited each year in their "Hagadah" (the story of Passover) "Leshana Habaa Bejerushalayim" (next year we will be in Jerusalem).

The trucks with dimmed headlights were exactly on time. We were all lined up and jumped onto the platform, eager to go. We were instructed to be silent the rest of the trip in order not to attract any attention to us. Once we were on the way I couldn't help but reminisce by comparison the trip I was making now to the trip I was making with my father on the German trucks from the Shrodula Ghetto to the Annaberg concentration camp. How I wished my father were with me now! Just thinking of all that had transpired since then made my head spin. The tarps were covered on all sides; no one could see in or out of the truck. I fell into a deep sleep, only to be awakened by Lolek telling me that we had to get off the truck. It was still dark outside when I realized that we were at the seashore, lined up to board a ship.

Lanegev. It was the town of Seth, a small Spanish fishing town just south of the French border, which served as the Haganah's staging ground of a large fishing boat of about 750 ton to ferry 750 enthusiastic youngsters to the Promised Land. The line was moving quickly; everybody was aware that time was of the essence. We had to get aboard the vessel before daybreak to evade being discovered by British intelligence. Inside the ship we were packed onto bunks tighter than sardines. Members of the Haganah were in charge of the operation. As soon as the ship was boarded, it took off into the sea. We were all assembled under the deck to be given the following orders: No one was allowed on deck during daylight hours. Plastic barfing bags were issued with instructions that they be tied tightly after use and disposed of into specified steel drums. Food and drinks would be served in pre-packed rations. All wrappings and disposal items must be deposited in specified containers for that purpose. There were only three toilets each for boys and girls. The cue for the toilets must be kept in an orderly fashion without quarrels. We were told that the name of this ship was Lanegev (onto the desert), symbolizing the importance of settling the arid land and turning it into agricultural production.

We were told that the Aegean Sea was very choppy during the winter. People would get seasick and vomit. They urged that people who were not affected by seasickness help those who were and maintain cleanliness and proper hygiene at all times. They announced that there would be a scheduled rotation period for each group when they could be on deck during the night and for how much time. Youngsters of all Zionist movements were on this ship, ranging from the ultra orthodox to the secular, from the far right to the far left, all representing the gamut of Jewish society of post-WWII Europe. We all shared a common goal: to go to the Promised Land. The spirit and enthusiasm of everyone aboard the ship was very high. We knew that we were making a valiant stand and a historical statement to the entire world. We would no longer tolerate the spilling of Jewish Blood! We would be the masters of our own destiny in our ancestral land! We would go to the Promised Land! In spite of the blockade of our shores set up by the British Empire, we would do what it took to exercise our right to return to our ancestral home.

Conditions on the ship were extremely crowded. Many people could not take the motion of the ocean and had to vomit. Fortunately, I was not suffering much from motion sickness. I arranged my schedule to sleep during the day so that I could have the time at night to go up on deck. It felt great to be on the deck with the stars reflecting from the ocean and the breeze blowing in my face. Many of the youngsters braved the ocean sickness and danced the Horah and other folk dances on the deck during all hours of the night. On many occasions, I had to take care of people vomiting uncontrollably. The euphoria of finally reaching the goal after all these years of anticipation, kept me vibrant and alive. Nothing could hinder me from enjoying every moment of it, not even the temporary setbacks of overcrowding and motion sickness.

I had the end result in mind. When would we reach the shores of Palestine? We were now 12 days into our voyage. The emissaries from the Haganah conducted meetings on the deck, preparing us for the critical moment when we reached the shores of Palestine. They told us point blank that it was highly unlikely that we would not be detected by the British Naval armada enforcing a blockade along the shores of Palestine. If we were lucky enough not to be detected, we would disembark from the ship as fast as we could as soon as it hit the sand on the shore. We were to run to the nearest Kibbutz for shelter. The most likely scenario was that the British Navy would intercept our ship once it got into the territorial waters, about 12 miles from the shoreline. They would escort the ship to the port of Haifa where they would forcefully board the ship. They would forcefully transfer all the passengers onto a British ship and take them to the detention camps in Cyprus. If this happened, there would be no point in forceful resistance. We must all gather on the deck of the ship in a peaceful protest and sing the "Hatikvah" (the Hebrew National Anthem). This so that the world can bear witness to the cruel ways in which the British were treating the survivors of the Holocaust.

On the night of the 14th day of the voyage, we could clearly see the lights on the shore of Palestine. We were jubilantly rejoicing at the sight of the shore when suddenly three British warships surrounded our ship and commandeered it to the port of Haifa. Since we were forewarned about this possible sequence of events, I quickly ran down to my bunk to collect my belongings and went running back onto the deck. At this point the ship was anchored and the British Navy boarded our ship.

All 750 of us were on top of the deck standing at attention. We started singing the Hatikvah, the Hebrew National Anthem, while the international media was photographing and recording the entire scene. The British used high-pressure water hoses to disperse the assembled crowd. They started forcing people onto navy vessels. A fellow standing next to me who spoke English told me what to say to the British soldier when he gets at me. I of course was happy to oblige even when I had no idea of what the meaning of the words were. When the British soldier came over to grab me, I called him a nasty name! He responded by shoving his rifle butt into my forehead. I figured that this would be a good time for me to faint; maybe they would take me to a local hospital? I fell to the ground, faking a fainting spell. They poured a bucket of ice water on my head. This certainly got me up in a hurry! They grabbed me and dragged me onto their ship headed for Cyprus. This was the price I paid for my first English lesson.

Famagusta, Cyprus. This was a sprawling WWII English military camp the British had converted into a detention camp for thousands of Jewish Holocaust survivors in their quest to reach the Promised Land. This act by the British government was in total contradiction of the Balfour declaration of November 2, 1917, in which Sir Arthur James Balfour, the British Foreign Secretary, had declared that Great Britain would favorably view the establishment of a Jewish National Home in Palestine. The British had the mandate of controlling large sections of the Arabian Peninsula and the Middle East that were taken away from Turkish domination. In the post-WWII era, when the world's dependence on oil from Arab countries had increased, the British government deemed it necessary to sell out all moral and ethical principles in order to carry favor with the Arab Sheikdoms of the Middle East and their oil. The Arab countries of the Middle East opposed Jewish migration and settlement in Palestine.

Inside the British detention camps of Cyprus, life and the pursuit of national goals were advanced by the robust indoctrination of Zionism and the establishment of a Jewish National Home in Palestine. While the camps were administered by the British in terms of food, lodging and medical treatment, the interior of the camps were exclusively run and governed by members of the Zionist organization of Palestine, the Haganah and the Irgun. The Zionists had total autonomy in the camps. The teaching curriculum evolved around practical necessities of daily life as pioneers in a hostile environment. Along with the general subjects of high school, we were given paramilitary training by members of the Haganah who had been sent to Cyprus specifically for that purpose. We were kept busy from dawn to dusk, and in addition, we had night exercises.

Our daily routine consisted of getting up at 6:00 a.m., having a 5-mile jog followed by a 45-minute judo session, after which we were allowed to have breakfast. We had normal school sessions during the day with an hour break for lunch. School ended at 4:30 in the afternoon, giving us an hour and a half to do our homework. Dinner was served at 6:00 p.m. At 7:00 p.m. we had night orientation classes during which we were taught to navigate by the stars. We had tunnels underneath the barbed wire fence leading outside of the camp. Our nightly excursions consisted of several groups going for a few miles in different directions with the objective of meeting at a central point two hours later. It was a great exercise in familiarizing ourselves with night conditions in varied terrain. Our instructors told us that there were many tactical advantages to night warfare. I found that to be true later on. While we did not have weapons in Cyprus, we used stones to simulate hand grenades in our exercises. All instructions and directions were given in Hebrew.

After meeting all qualifying requirements of the training course, we were given the honor and the privilege to be sworn in as members of the Haganah. We were sitting on the ground in a large dark tent. In front of us was a raised platform with a white curtain drawn across it. Behind the curtain was a table with three chairs, where our military instructors were seated. As they called every student for the swearing-in ceremony, you could see the shadow of the student on the white curtain as he or she was holding a gun in his or her right hand and the palm of the left hand laid on the bible while each individual was being sworn into the Haganah. It was extremely exciting and emotionally rewarding to take part in this swearing-in ceremony.

After the ceremony we lit a fire and danced the night away starting with Hora and ending up with all sorts of folk dances. The next morning at 6 a.m. sharp we got up for the jog. During the judo session, the trainer had us lay down on the ground and asked us to harden and strain our belly muscles. He would then jump from belly to belly without touching ground (he did it in his bare feet). This was hard to take at first, but as time went on, we built up our belly muscles and got used to it. The training got increasingly harder as we gained greater proficiency in a variety of military maneuvers. The training included the build up of physical stamina and crossing of all sorts of obstacles, such as ravines and narrow rivers.

In July 1947 we practiced river crossing on ropes that stretched over a span of 50 feet at a height of 22 feet. This involved crawling across the span with a backpack and getting off at the other end on a dangling rope. I was unable to make it across to the end and let my feet dangle down. My instructor asked me to get my feet back up and make it across to the end. I was not able to do it, so he finally asked me to jump down onto the ground. I fractured my left leg during the jump and was taken to the hospital in Famagusta, Cyprus, where they put my leg in a cast. All my buddies had a field day signing the cast. I was unable to partake in all the activities. I took up stone carving during my spare time. I enjoyed it; it helped pass the time.

There was a lot of pressure being exerted on the British government to ease some of the restrictions on the Holocaust survivors detained in the camps in Cyprus. Her Majesty, the Queen of England, relented, and in an act of generosity allowed 500 orphaned Holocaust survivors to immigrate to Palestine. Because I had a fractured leg, I was chosen to be among the 500 orphans scheduled to leave for Palestine by August the 23rd. As it happened, my cast was taken off on the 18th of August and I was still on the departure list. The idea of being in the Promised Land for my 18th birthday was the best birthday gift I could think of. I was delighted and could not wait to leave.

Negba. On the evening of the 22nd of August, we were informed that our entire group would be able to join the transport to Palestine the next morning. We were overjoyed and spent the entire night celebrating and dancing. It wasn't until the wee hours of the morning that we gathered our belongings quickly to line up for the trip. As we lined up, we noticed that there were other groups of various affiliations lined up for the trip as well. All of the groups were exuberantly celebrating their trip to the Promised Land. Eitan, our trainer from the Haganah, was with us and asked us to keep a lid on our celebrations. He informed us that there were major discussions in the international leadership regarding the establishment of a Jewish National Home in Palestine. He explained to us that this was a crucial time in our quest to attain international recognition of our rights to settle and establish a Jewish National Home in the land of our forefathers. We were all so concentrated on attaining our goal that this is the kind of discussion we had while waiting to board the buses to go to Famagusta.

At the port of Famagusta, we were met by an army of photographers and newspaper reporters from the British and International press, publicizing the act of generosity by her Majesty, the Queen of England, allowing 500 orphans of the Holocaust to go to Palestine. We just wanted to board the ship and get on our way. When the anchors were lifted and the ship was in motion, we all started to cheer. The British soldiers on the ship were nice and polite; they served us food and goodies while we were impatiently waiting to reach the shores of Palestine. As soon as we sighted land, all 500 of us got onto the deck to witness the moment. As soon as the marines dropped their anchors and the ship stopped moving, we all stood at attention and burst out singing the Hatikvah. It was one of the most memorable moments of my life.

Mount Carmel overlooking the Haifa harbor looked so beautifully majestic. Tears were running down my face while waiting to board the bus. Eitan, our Haganah trainer, was pointing out the various towns to us as we were traveling south through Herzeliah, Tel-Aviv, Jaffa, Rechovot, until we finally arrived after an hour and forty-five minutes drive to Negba (South).

Negba was a kibbutz (communal settlement), located south of Rechovot and east of Ashdod. The members of Negba were secular in their beliefs, and their political orientation was that of Hashomer Hatzair (The Young Guardian), which was socialist. It must be noted that most of the Jewish settlements throughout the Holy Land were communal or cooperative in structure, regardless of their political affiliation. The reason for that was safety and protection from Arab marauders. There were kibbutzim with political orientation ranging from the far right to the far left. Most of the kibbutzim, however, were secular in their persuasion and were strong supporters and adherents of the Haganah (the Jewish defense forces). There were kibbutzim of the far right movement that relied on protection from the Irgun (an ultra right militant organization).

Negba was located between the main highway leading from Tel-Aviv to Gaza on the west and the crossroad leading from Gaza eastward to Jerusalem. The police compound known as Iraq El Suidan, which was built by the British, was located on a hill with a strategically commanding view of Negba and the surrounding road junctions. It served and was used as a British police station to enforce the rules and regulations of the British mandate. The management of the kibbutz and its members maintained a cooperative relationship with the police station command and personnel.

Negba was a self-contained agricultural kibbutz whose members were hard-working idealists pursuing the Zionist goal. They all came from Eastern European countries and settled in this arid land and turned into a productive agricultural enterprise. Our arrival in Negba constituted an infusion of young new blood into the system. Our integration into the community was meticulously planned. We were assigned a first-rate teaching staff and instructors to facilitate our smooth assimilation into the community.

Our schedule was split between study, work, and military training. The studies were necessary in order for us to complete all the subjects for high school matriculation. We were required to take a fast course in Hebrew language and literature in order to improve our communication skills in Hebrew. We worked in the fields and cow stables. We acquired the skills necessary to sustain a vibrant, progressive hard-working community. The military training was essential because of the threats proclaimed against the Jewish community in Palestine by many leaders of neighboring Arab countries as well as by the Grand Mufti of Jerusalem.

We trained together with the boys and girls that were born in Negba and vicinity. This served as an important catalyst to rapid integration. Despite our hectic schedule, we kept up with local as well as international news. We were especially interested in the deliberations taking place in the newly formed United Nations Assembly in New York. The Jewish community all over the world, and the Zionist organizations in particular, were fully aware that the guilt complex of the Western World for the killing of six million Jews while they were standing idly by, would only last so long. Now was the time for us to ask them to act and right the wrong that was perpetrated against us. Now was the time for us to press them to vote for the establishment of a Jewish National Home when it came up for a vote at the United Nations.

The newspapers and radio broadcasts were keeping the topic alive in front of the entire world. At last, a vote on the subject was scheduled for November 29, 1947. The jubilation and anticipation of the Jewish community in Palestine as well as elsewhere in the world was beyond words. There was dancing and singing everywhere. Polls were taken back and forth if the measure will pass in the UN assembly. There was a lot of excitement and anticipation everywhere. Preparations were made for us to listen to the deliberations and vote in the large mess hall of the kibbutz on the 29th of November. There is a 10-hour difference between New York and Tel-Aviv, which meant that we might have to stay up all night to hear the results of the vote. The Jewish communities from around the world set up lobbying committees to bring influence to bear

157

on a favorable vote for the establishment of a Jewish State. The text of resolution 181 before the United Nations actually was to establish a Jewish and an Arab state side by side in Palestine. On November the 29th, right after dinner was served, the tables were put aside and chairs were set up in rows for us to be able to bear witness to this historic moment. From what I heard on the radio broadcasts, Jewish communities throughout the entire world were clinging to their radios to listen to the deliberations.

The speeches were going on and on. It was dawn when the voting began. The final results of the vote were: 33 in favor of Resolution 181, 13 votes against the resolution, and 10 abstentions, to establish a Jewish and an Arab state, side by side, in Palestine. When the final vote was announced, we jumped for joy, forming a circle, dancing and singing.

The sad part of the vote was that all the Arab countries rejected the vote outright even though the resolution read to "establish a Jewish state and an Arab state, side by side." This was a clear sign of an ominous threat to our existence as a people and as a nation. It meant that we were now facing threats from the North, South and East, as well as within Palestine itself from the forces of the Grand Mufti of Jerusalem. They all threatened to drive us into the Mediterranean Sea, which was on our west. The prospects for a peaceful resolution of the problem with the Arab states were nil. They were adamant about preventing the establishment of a Jewish state.

It was now left up to the Jewish National Council to meet with the British and set up a date by which the British would transfer the power and the new state would be born. It was fairly easy to set a date for when the British would leave Palestine. The date was set for May 15, 1948, which meant that the British would have to leave all their bases by midnight of May 14, 1948. The question now was, in what condition would the British leave the country to the protagonists. As the weeks and months went by, the British made it abundantly clear that they favored the Arabs over the Jews. They transferred to the Arabs all strategic locations on the high grounds that controlled the transportation arteries between Tel-Aviv and Jerusalem and between Gaza and Jerusalem. Not only did they turn over these strategically located police stations to the Arabs, they left all the weapons and ammunition in these stations for the Arabs so that they could use them to fight the Jews.

The paramount interest of the British was what oil concessions they could get from the Arabs by giving them an enormous territorial advantage in their quest to drive the Jews into the Mediterranean sea. All of the surrounding Arab countries, including the Grand Mufti of Jerusalem, vowed to drive the Jews into the ocean. The British were sure that the Jewish population of Palestine wouldn't stand a chance to survive an all-out assault by the armada of all the surrounding Arab armies. They surely did their best to assure them success. They handed over to the Arabs the Latrun Police station that controlled the cross roads from Tel Aviv to Jerusalem, thereby denying access to the Jewish capital. There were numerous instances where the British violated their neutrality in transferring the territories in accordance to United Nations directives. While the official date to transfer sovereignty was May 15th, 1948, hostilities started in various areas immediately after the UN vote was taken. The period of December 1, 1947, to May 15, 1948, was used by the Arabs to probe the weaknesses in the Jewish communities of Palestine in preparation for an all-out assault.

We did not just stand idly by. In Negba, we took hectic measures to prepare ourselves and the area for defending ourselves in case of an attack. We built a chain of trenches and bunkers around our perimeter. We erected a barbed wire fence all around it. We did everything within our power to secure our homes and property within the legal boundaries of the British mandate. Our military training now included the use of incendiary devices, Molotov cocktails, and hand grenades. We prepared the ground in front of our fences to be mined in case of an infantry attack against our forward positions.

The problem was that while the surrounding Arab countries were arming themselves preparing for the onslaught, the Jews were prevented by the rules of the British mandate from importing any weapons or ammunition. This not only put us at a great disadvantage, it forced us to concentrate on defensive measures in the hope that we would hold back the Arab on-

Sam Silberberg

slaught until after we declared our independence. We must
make worldwide purchases of weapons and ammunition to
reach our beleaguered forces right after independence is declared. Our entire existence was based on a gamble that the
Jewish community of Palestine would be able to resist and
hold off the Arab onslaught until such time that the newly
purchased weapons would arrive.

The Haganah had many seasoned soldiers from the Jewish
Brigade of WWII. They fought with the African corps with the
British against the German field marshal Rommel. They were
in charge of all the planning and implementation of the military strategies in the event of an attack. The Haganah, in con-
junction with the World wide Zionist organization, purchased
weapons and ammunition from weapons manufacturers
around the world, especially Czechoslovakia, to arrive in the
Jewish state right after the declaration of independence.

All these events were taking place during this interim period.
There was no more time to study; all our efforts were directed
towards the moment when we would declare our independence. It was a hectic time, laden with anxiety about the outcome of the battle. In my heart I knew that this time I would
stand and fight with my colleagues like a tiger to defend the
right of our people to live as free men in our ancestral homeland. Never again will Jews go like sheep to the slaughterhouse! We will fight for our right! We worked extended hours
to make sure that we achieved the maximum defensible security to our perimeter.

On May 14, 1948, the last day of the British rule of Palestine,
the Egyptians didn't wait for the official declaration of independence. Their air force attacked us and dropped incendiary
bombs on our haystacks and strafed our cow stables, killing
several cows. We got the message. We realized that the situation was too dangerous for our children to be around in a
combat zone. The children and their staff were evacuated to
the interior of the country. In deference of the religious feelings of many Jews, the council leaders decided to make the
declaration of independence before sun down on Friday the
14th in order not to desecrate the Jewish Sabbath. We sat in
complete silence as David Ben-Gurion, the leader of the Jew-

160

ish Council of Palestine, proclaimed the establishment of an independent Jewish state in **Eretz Israel** (The Land of Israel). We all stood at attention and sang the "Hatikvah" (The Israeli National Anthem).

I remember hugging my girlfriend Gilah Davidowicz. I was happy to share with her this historical moment of our lives. Tears of happiness were running down both of our cheeks. Gilah was also my companion in the trenches defending the perimeter of position #5 to which we were assigned. The entire perimeter of Negba was divided into defensive positions. Gilah, myself and two other boys were responsible for the defense of position #5 under my command.

The Arab nations surrounding Israel didn't even wait for the official expiration time of the British mandate. They were determined not to share the possibility of two independent states living side by side in peaceful coexistence. They were determined to eliminate the Jewish state. As a matter of fact, they were so sure that they would chase the Jews into the sea that they urged the Arab residents of Palestine to leave their homes for a short duration, during which the Arab armies would achieve victory. The residents would then return to their homes and share in the booty of the vanquished Jewish residents. The British also were sure that a community of only 650,000 Jews could not possibly hold back an armada of millions of Arabs.

There was no way the Jews could survive such an onslaught. These dire predictions were made by the British, knowing that they would not allow the Jews to import any weapons or ammunitions. Not only that, they knew that they were giving the Arabs key strategic advantages over the Jews. There would be no logical or logistic reason why the Arabs couldn't triumph within a short period of time. As a matter of fact, the Arabs made stunning gains within the first few days of their invasion. The Arab Legion of Trans-Jordan was able to cut off Jerusalem from the rest of the country. The Egyptian army cut off the entire Negev desert right at the crossroad north of us and occupied the police station of Iraq-el-Suweidan. The Syrians and Lebanese in the north were pushing southward. It was a bleak picture. None of it, however, would dampen our spirit and determination.

Negba was clearly under the guns of Egyptian artillery. Egyptian airplanes were attacking us daily. All we could do was dig in deeper into our trenches. When the Egyptians occupied Gaza and went north along the coast, we were concerned that we, too, may be cut off. They decided to attack and clean out settlements along the way. They attacked and took over the kibbutz of Yad Mordechai, which was northeast of Gaza. We knew that we were going to be attacked next, because they shelled and harassed us constantly. The Haganah sent an expeditionary force and tried one night to attack and take over the police station of Iraq-el-Suweidan, with no success.

The reason for a night attack was simple: we had a very small force with limited firepower. At night we were able to place loud speakers and sparklers in different spots giving the illusion of a large force and take advantage of the element of surprise which could not be done in daylight. The main thrust on the police compound was performed by commando units. They were unable to penetrate the fortress like police station and had to retreat.

On June 2, 1948, the Egyptians shelled our positions for six hours without a stop. Their planes flew several sorties over our heads strafing the entire area with a blanket of fire. They followed it with a column of armored tanks moving towards our positions and shelling from their turrets. As soon as they came over our minefields, their tanks were disabled and their attack came to a halt and retreated. We lost 8 of our defenders in that attack, while the Egyptians left over a hundred bodies strewn all over the battle field and our mine fields.

We learned two important lessons from this encounter: do not open fire until their infantry reaches our minefields, and be ready to use hand grenades and Molotov cocktails only after they breach our fences.

The practicality of these lessons was simple: we were limited with our ammunition; we had to use them in the most effective way. Another important observation was that we realized that the Egyptian soldiers were not motivated to fight for the Palestinians and give up their lives for them.

There were several other indications of miscommunication between the attacking forces and their commanders. Their artillery fire kept exploding on their advancing troops and killing them. The first battle tested our ability to hold our positions and repel the attacking forces. We had to be fully prepared for more attacks.

On the night of June 11, while I was taking a nap in the bunker, Gilah was on guard duty, sitting on top of the trench. I heard the thud of an enemy artillery shell being fired. As soon as I started yelling for Gilah to take cover, the shell exploded right in front of our trench.

גילה דוידוביץ

Gilah Davidovitz, my girlfriend,
who was fatally wounded in an attack.

Gilah was hit by shrapnel. The medics rushed her to the first aid station, where she died. Her aorta had been severed by a piece of shrapnel, causing her to bleed to death.

Soon thereafter, the Egyptians unleashed a steady barrage of artillery fire from Gaza and Migdal to our west. While their forces at the police station were shelling us with 3-inch mortar batteries, the sky above us was abuzz with flickering shells falling and exploding all around us. When the skies started to get light amidst all this shelling, we noticed that there were hundreds of enemy tanks rolling from the police station towards us. We immediately telephoned our commanders to inform them of the situation on the ground. They ordered us to stay calm and under cover watch them advance. We were not to open fire on them until after their infantry units were on our minefields.

The problem was that the Egyptian artillery, in an attempt to cover the advance of their forces, kept shelling on their own troops on the minefields. It was difficult for us to tell, watching their dying infantry troops, whether it was as a result of them tripping our mines, their artillery killing them, or the fire of our machine guns. It was a scene of total carnage. Explosions were heard all over the battlefield terrain, everything was full of smoke and fire; the smell of gunpowder was permeating the air. The Egyptian tanks kept pressing forward, moving towards our perimeter, even at the cost of trampling their own wounded soldiers to death. The onslaught was so steady and relentless that one of the Egyptian tanks managed to break through our fence at position #6 which was on our left about 75 feet from our position. The crew of position #6 tossed a few Molotov cocktails on the tank setting it on fire. The heat of the burning steel caused the tank crew to jump out of the tank. As they jumped out from the escape hutch, our crews shot them.

The battle was intense, and my adrenalin was running extremely high. I didn't even feel that I was injured. When I wiped the sweat off my forehead, I realized that it was red. Only when I tried to take my helmet off, I felt a sharp pain. Shrapnel had hit my helmet, causing a sharp edge to injure my head. There was no way I could leave the battlefield with a breach of our perimeter to the left of our position. I called in the medic who bandaged me up. While the medic was attending to my wound, all the explosions stopped and a sudden stillness prevailed. We were wondering what had happened? Looking over the battlefield, we saw all these tanks retreating and leaving the dead and injured behind with smoke rising from the scorched earth.

We fought a very hard battle, considering the overwhelming force that attacked us. The Egyptians lost 400 soldiers, while we lost 10 defenders, including Gilah. In addition to the dead bodies, the Egyptians left behind some of their injured soldiers in our minefields. It was unfortunate that we could not help the injured, because it was too risky for our medics to go into the minefields. Now we had to bury our dead defenders. Gilah, along with two other comrades from the kibbutz, were buried in a common grave known as the grave of the brave defenders of Negba, while the other bodies were sent to their families for burial services.

In the aftermath of the battle, I felt the pain and sorrow of loosing Gilah. I started questioning if this loss had been avoidable and if there was anything I could have done to prevent it. This seemed to evoke the same feelings of guilt and reasoning I had when I lost my father. It seems that we are a product of our Judeo Christian heritage where guilt feelings are so deeply rooted in our traditions that we allow them to play havoc with our lives.

Shmilek (me), age 19, in Negba, Israel. 1948

The aftermath of the big battle gave us pause to assess and evaluate our actions during the fight for our survival. We were proud, as was the rest of the Israeli nation, that we were able to repulse an enemy attack of this magnitude with such great odds against us. This was an extremely difficult period for the nation as a whole. In its infancy, it was attacked from all sides by an overwhelming force trying to wipe it off the map. Unless we would receive a reprieve of some sort to be able to catch our breath, we would not last.

That reprieve came in the form of a United Nations-enforced ceasefire, which took effect on June 11, 1948. During that ceasefire, weapons and ammunitions purchased by financial contributions from Jewish organizations in the USA and the rest of the world arrived in Israeli ports. The newly formed Israeli government, in close cooperation with Jewish and Christian organizations from all over the world, made strenuous efforts to purchase military equipment and weapons for the beleaguered state of Israel.

Czechoslovakia was one of the countries that supplied Israel with modern machine guns and armaments from the factories that the Germans had left behind during WWII. While most of the world was sympathetic to the success and survival of the fledgling state of Israel, the British government still maintained a de facto boycott of military equipment to Israel.

During that ceasefire, I was given a one-week furlough to make a trip to Jerusalem. Jerusalem was beleaguered and cut off from the rest of the country by the Arab Legion of Trans-Jordan at the main crossroad of the Latrun (name of a town) Police station. The control of this crossing was handed over to the Arab Legion by Britain. No civilian traffic was allowed between Jerusalem and the rest of the country. Only military and supply vehicles were allowed passage. That passage was created by an alternate route cut through the rocks of the Judean hills by the Israeli army corps of engineers. The road was called Kvish Nachshon (the serpentine road).

I made it a practice to mail the letters to my mother from Tel Aviv. I did not want her to know and worry that I was in the midst of a war zone. This time, I was informing her of my trip to Jerusalem visiting a second cousin who lived there.

I was unable to visit my grandfather's grave on the Mount of Olives, because that section of Jerusalem, as well as the Old City and the Holy places, were captured by the Arab Legions of Trans-Jordan. This was my first letter to my mother after the ceasefire; I wanted her to know that I was alive and well. I went into our tomato fields and picked a crate full of fresh tomatoes to bring to my cousin Zemach Silberberg.

The trip was quite an adventure. I had to first go to Rehovot, where the convoy for the trip to Jerusalem was being assembled, to join the military escort. I was excited to finally have a chance to see the capital of Israel, Jerusalem. I had been shlepping (dragging along) my military gear with a crate of tomatoes when I was assigned to one of the supply trucks in the convoy to beleaguered Jerusalem. Escorting troops were standing on the stoop of the cabin, ready to jump off and take defensive positions in case of an attack. We were armed with a rifle and a belt of hand grenades. Once we reached the serpentine road in total darkness, the trucks in the convoy were not allowed to turn on their headlights. The convoy literally crawled the rest of the night, bobbing up and down throughout the entire serpentine stretch. It wasn't until dawn that we connected again with the main road to Jerusalem.

I was impressed by the architectural integrity of the buildings of the city of Jerusalem. They were constructed with native yellow stone carved out of the Judean hills surrounding Jerusalem. As the sun hit the buildings, they had a golden reflection, giving them that unique feeling that is "Jerusalem of Gold."

When I arrived at my cousin's house I remembered that he was an ultra orthodox Chasidic Jew. He found my secular convictions abhorrent and untenable. We agreed to disagree and not to engage in discussions of religion and politics. My main reason for going to Jerusalem was to find out the circumstances under which my grandfather had died in 1942. I had very warm feelings for him. I remembered him praying at the hospital for my recovery. I remembered the bon-voyage party in the fall of 1938 that was given in his honor. I know that my reason for being here was because of the spark of Zionism that uncle Moses ignited in me during that party. I remembered the Kaddish (mourning prayer) in his memory during which I escaped from the Death March. I attributed the success of that escape to his divine intervention, even though I was not a believer.

I regretted the fact that I could not pay my respects at his gravesite, which was now occupied by the Jordanian army. I would have liked to be able to visit all the historical sites in the old city of Jerusalem, but they, too, were occupied by the Jordanian army.

Hungarian Youth Group fighting in Negba.
I am the second person from the left in the front row.

I made arrangements with the military command to return as an escort through the serpentine road to my base in Negba.

Sam Silberberg

Water tower of Negba, shattered by Egyptian artillery.

Hungarian Youth Group, fighting in Negba, Israel (1948)

The return trip to Negba was substantially faster, because the trucks were empty. We still had to travel in total darkness, which was extremely dangerous on those steep curves. Upon returning to Negba, I learned that many members of the Palmach unit (special forces unit) were called in for a special action to the shores of Herzliya, a town north of Tel Aviv. Their mission was to prevent the ship Altalena, which was loaded with weapons and ammunition destined for the Irgun, a right-wing military organization, from unloading its cargo. The leadership of Israel, headed by Ben-Gurion, decided that there could not be a splintered military authority in the country.

Haganah, the Israeli defense forces, under the direction of the central government, was the only military force responsible for the security of the country. The Irgun, which was operating independently in operations against the British and during the interim period between the UN resolution and the official declaration of the State of Israel, could no longer operate as a separate military entity in total disregard of the interests of the State of Israel. The units of the Palmach and Haganah had to make sure that members of the Irgun on the ship Altalena did not disembark with their weapons.

The Altalena was moored in the Tel Aviv Harbor, and its members disembarked, leaving the weapons and ammunition on the ship. The ship was unloaded, and the weapons were integrated into the Israeli Defense Forces (IDF). This was the closest the Israeli nation came to a civil war. Ben-Gurion was credited with preventing a rift and civil strife in the newly created nation of Israel. The ceasefire period was used very effectively by the state of Israel.

The vast purchases of weapons and military equipment began to arrive in our ports and were immediately distributed to crucial battlefields across Israel. We were given instructions in the use of new machine guns and 3-inch mortar equipment as well as advanced communication equipment. Looking back at the state of our armament prior to the first ceasefire, I couldn't help but wonder how we could repel an attack of such overwhelming force.

The answer to this, in simple Hebrew, was "Ein breira" (There is no choice.). Was it really as simple as that? True, we had no alternative but to fight for our right to have a place in the sun. But there was more to it than that. We, the survivors of the Holocaust, were carrying the burden of 2,000 years of Jewish persecution in the Diaspora on our shoulders.

The creation of the State of Israel had a meaning and a reason for our survival. This is why we had the determination and were able to clench our fists and fight a heroic battle. We had the courage of our convictions, we had the emotional and intellectual strength to endure what it took in order to show the world, "Yes, we can do it! We proved that we could." We knew where we came from, and we were determined to claim back our birth right in the land of our forefathers, The Promised Land.

It was not at all surprising that the armada of the entire Arab populations in the Middle East could not defeat us. These poor soldiers were in the servitude of a feudal system whose corrupt rulers denied them their basic rights and freedoms as human beings and citizens. They lacked will, determination, and most of all, a reason to fight a war that was forced on them by corrupt rulers. Yet, because of the massive, overwhelming force in both numbers and weaponry, they were able to separate the Negev, which is the southern part of Israel, and Jerusalem, which is the capital, from the mainland. The ceasefire gave us the respite needed to regroup and recuperate from the loss of friends and loved ones. It also enabled us to rearm and train our forces with new and up-to-date weaponry. During the entire ceasefire period, we were smuggling weapons and supplies to the beleaguered Negev.

In the darkness of night, our scouts would lead convoys of soldiers carrying weapons and ammunition through enemy lines into the beleaguered Negev. The route used for this purpose was from Negba, going between the crossroad and the Iraq El Suidan police station to the Negev. It worked out well, because we were trained for night warfare. We used the night and our familiarity with the terrain to lead the convoys to the Negev and to prepare them for a joint counter attack.

On July 8, 1948, the ceasefire was broken by the Jordanian forces of the Arab Legion near the Latrun junction to Jerusalem. This violation of the ceasefire opened a window of opportunity for the Israeli Defense Forces, who had been retrofitting the entire military with daily shipments of new armaments, to go on the offensive. The Arab armies were keeping a strangle hold on the Jewish nation by splintering off the

Negev desert to the south and Jerusalem the capital of the newborn State of Israel in the southeast. It was now the task of the Israeli Defense Forces to turn a leaf and go on the offense to free the chokehold the enemy had on the Negev and Jerusalem. On the southern front, the Israeli Defense Forces, in coordination with the reinforced and rearmed troops of the Negev desert, mounted an attack on the main cross roads, leading from Gaza to Jerusalem, which was controlled by the Iraq El Suidan police fortress.

This attack took place in the middle of the night when decoy units could be staged to confuse the enemy. In line with this plan, a decoy attack was staged on the Iraq El Suidan fortress, while the main objective was to occupy the crossroads and cut off the Egyptian forces from their command headquarters in Gaza, thereby controlling the road to the Negev desert. The operation succeeded. We reached our objective after several hours of intense fighting. We took control of the crossroads, uniting the Negev desert with the rest of the country. We cut off the Egyptian army east of the crossroads from their source of supply in Gaza. These Egyptian forces were under the command of Colonel Gamel Abdel Nasser, who later became the president of Egypt. These troops were now isolated and surrounded without any sources of supply. On the Latrun junction, which controlled the main highway to Jerusalem, the situation was a lot more difficult. The Arab Legion of Trans-Jordan controlled the heights of the area from the Latrun Police Fortress. They were disciplined soldiers, trained and well supplied by the British Army. The Royal Air Force, as well as the British officers were planning and directing their operations.

The Israeli Defense Forces (IDF) suffered enormous casualties in lives and equipment in the battles of Latrun. The rocky Judean hills, combined with the British-installed radar warning system, made it difficult and costly to launch a surprise attack. The IDF were pouring in wave after wave of attacking infantry until, at last, they managed to capture the intersection of the main highway to Jerusalem, the capital of the newly created State of Israel. Still, the intersection was under constant threat of gunfire and mortars from the fortress of Latrun, which was held by the Arab Legion. It was one of the hardest and costliest battles fought in the war of independence of the State of Israel in 1948. When the second ceasefire was announced by the United Nations, Israel was in possession of the main crossroads to Jerusalem and had united the Negev desert with the mainland. At this stage, weapons and ammunitions were arriving daily in Israeli ports, buttressing the gains made by the IDF. Now there was no doubt that we had gained the upper hand on the ground. It was only a question of time before some pockets of resistance would be cleared up.

When the second ceasefire was violated by the Arab nations, Israel was ready to reclaim all the ground lost during the first phase of the attacks. The IDF secured the approach to the Jerusalem main highway, capturing the high ground and the Latrun police fortress. The IDF launched a concentrated attack on the Iraq El Suidan fortress and finally captured it. We went up on the roof of the Iraq El Suidan Fortress after it was captured. Looking down from top of the roof, Negba looked like it was in the palm of their hand. No wonder they attacked us with such an overwhelming force, trying to eliminate us. The United Nations negotiated the withdrawal of the encircled Egyptian army in Feludgia (east of the Iraq El Suidan fortress) that was commanded by colonel Gamed Abdel Nasser. The troops were allowed to leave the area without their weapons or ammunition.

With the retreat of the Egyptian army from Feludgia, everything was peaceful. Life in Negba returned to normal, the children and their staff returned to the Kibbutz, the fields and life stock were attended to as usual. There was a lot of rebuilding to be done. The concrete water tower was punctured with holes and could no longer be used. Damaged homes and cow stables had to be repaired. Most of the infrastructure was damaged by artillery shells and bombs and needed rebuilding. The void in my heart caused by Gilah's absence was a lot more difficult to repair. I was given a variety of tasks and responsibilities to perform, which helped to alleviate some of the sadness over Gilah's death. The kibbutz (communal settlement) returned to its normal schedule of meetings and deliberations. The topic of deliberations ranged from economic development of the kibbutz to deciding which of the children to send to college.

I was struck by the vote and criteria by which some children should be subsidized and sent to college. I fully understood that that the community did not have enough funds to send all the children to college. But the idea of other people voting and deciding whether or not my children could go to college made me wonder about the whole idea of a communal system. After mulling with the idea for a number of days, I came to the conclusion that if I had children of college age, I would not want someone else to decide if they were worthy of going to college. This notion soured my whole ideal of communal living and I began to have second thoughts about it. It triggered in me the whole process of evaluation and assessment regarding the idealism of a socialist communal society vs. a private enterprise society. I asked myself: how does the communal life of a group of 200 people differ from that of an individual? I posed this question in terms of a global solution for an idealistic society. I was reminded of the following quote by Winston Churchill: "If you are not an idealist at the age of 18, you've got no heart. If you are an idealist at the age of 40, you've got no brain." This pretty much settled the argument for me.

I started looking for ways in which I could, in good faith, leave the utopia of kibbutz life and fend for myself in a competitive free-enterprise society. The basic argument for doing so was that I had given and devoted a lot of energy to idealistic causes. Now was the time to test the waters and work for myself.

Setting up a Corporation. After several conversations with some of my colleagues, I realized that I was not the only one who felt that way about kibbutz life. There were five us who felt that this was the time to branch out and try something new. We set up a construction corporation that specialized in the erection of standardized, poured, concrete 50-head cow stables. Our system was based on a three-day turnaround time. We erected the forms with rebars, ready to pour in one day. We poured the concrete in the early morning hours of the second day. On the third day, we dismantled the forms and loaded them on a truck, ready for the next job. It was an efficiently designed standardized system that worked well. With the country's population increasing, there turned out to be a growing demand for our services.

We worked from dawn to dusk for over two years with this system. I was able to save money, because we ate and slept at the settlements and farms where we built these cow stables. I saved the money so that I could buy property to build a house and eventually settle down. Unfortunately, all this hard work and frugal living in order to gather enough money to buy me a piece of the Promised Land turned to naught overnight. The finance minister Dov Yosef, from Britain, decided to revamp the financial system and devalue the shekel by 90%, which killed my dreams to buy property and build a house.

As a result of this catastrophic devaluation, we had to dissolve the corporation and stop work on our projects. I was terribly upset and disillusioned with the leadership of the country and depressed that after two-and-a-half years of hard work I had nothing to show for it. I had no choice but to seek residence in the house of my cousin of the Poisson family in Ramat Gan, a suburb of Tel Aviv. I was thankful for their generosity in accepting me as part of their family with their two sons. I took a job as a framing carpenter with a local construction company. I was disillusioned and depressed about the devaluation and the havoc it played with people's lives.

I finally gave in to my mother's plea, who was in the USA, to visit her. However, obtaining a visa to the USA was hard and took more than six months. I had to first get my Israeli passport and then wait my turn to get a US visa to enter the United States of America.

My mother sent a beautiful thank you note to the Poissons for treating me as part of their family. I, too, thanked them for their generosity in accepting me into their home. My mother and my aunt Sarah arranged for me to fly to Rome in July 1952, visit with my aunt Sarah in Zeilsheim near Frankfurt in Germany, return to Italy and sail from the port of Naples to the United States on an Italian ship called Conte Biancamano

EPILOGUE

In mid July 1952, I flew to Rome, where I spent several days visiting sites. Then I took the train to Frankfurt to visit my aunt Sarah. She had married a cousin of ours, Shieka Wachsman, and had two children, Abe and Goldie. The train passed many beautiful lakes and meadows at the foot of the Alps. The scenery was breathtaking. At the end of my visit, my aunt decided to visit Italy together with me before my departure to the USA. We had a great time visiting Rome and southern Italy before I departed from Naples.

Shmilek and Aunt Sarah on the Isle of Capri, 1952

The voyage on the ship Conte Biancamano was enjoyable. There was delicious food and good entertainment. Upon arriving in New York, I was taken to Ellis Island for three days.

My mother was upset but recovered once I was released. We hugged and talked about my experiences in Israel and the reasons why I had come to the United States.

I enrolled in the Mergenthaler Linotype School in New York City to become a typesetter. I wanted to renew the family tradition of printing. Upon graduation, I took a job as a linotype operator in Clyde, Ohio, because I wanted to be in an English-speaking environment, where no other languages were spoken, in order to improve my English.

On my way to Clyde, Ohio, I stopped in Rochester, NY, to visit the Rochester Institute of Technology (RIT), an accredited college that offered a BS degree in printing. (I could not extend my visa status in the USA unless I enrolled in an accredited college). After an interview in the admissions office my application was declined. I felt let down and disappointed. On my way to the railroad station, I asked a man for directions to the station. He must have sensed that I was distraught. He asked if there was anything he could do for me and gave me his business card. His name was Lester Edelman, who worked for the *Democrat and Chronicle*, the local newspaper.

Once I settled in Clyde, I contacted Mr. Edelman to set up an appointment to meet with him during my Passover visit to my mother in New York. During that meeting, he arranged for an interview for me at RIT. I was admitted to the college during that interview.

I maintained contact with the Edelman family. While at RIT, I worked as a Hebrew and Jewish history teacher at Temple B'rith Kodesh, a reform temple in Rochester. Upon graduation, I worked as a production manager for several printing and publishing companies.

On February 22, 1958, I married my wife Anita Natzler. We have two children and two grandchildren. We celebrated our 50th wedding anniversary in 2008.

Made in the USA
Las Vegas, NV
26 May 2024

90382710R00105